MW00897853

CAPTIVATING STORIES

FOR CURIOUS KIDS

UNBELIEVABLE TALES FROM HISTORY, SCIENCE AND THE STRANGE WORLD WE LIVE IN

CHRIS MUNOZ

A SPECIAL GIFT TO SAY THANKS

Exclusive Bonus Chapters and Their Audio,
Created Just For You!

GO TO THE LAST PAGE TO CLAIM YOUR GIFT

TABLE OF CONTENTS

INTRODUCTION

Once there was a boy who wanted to be a man...

Once there was an ostrich who wanted its mate to come back to life...

Once there was a woman who thought she could do more with her life...

Once there was a mother who wanted her son back...

Once there was an octopus, quite content to be alone...

Once there was a man who learned to live with deformity...

Once there was a monkey that people thought was cursed...

"Once there was" can go on and on and on. This is the beauty of stories. New ones are being made every day, both fiction and nonfiction. This collection only shares what's true, though. The stories here will seek to inform you, entertain you, and make you think a little bit about the crazy world we live in. After you've taken a long look through its pages, perhaps you'll agree with the saying "truth is stranger than fiction".

Humans find some weird ways to entertain themselves. They throw oranges at each other. They perfect the art of sledding. They invent popsicles and earmuffs. They try to create phones to talk with the dead. They play pranks on each other. If you want to be entertained, read on.

There are also stories of accomplishments. The first recorded journey across the North American continent, perhaps largely led by a wife won in a poker game. The discovery of radiation. The self-made millionaire born to a family of slaves. If you want to be inspired, read on.

The animal kingdom hosts more stories than can be counted. Stories of rainbow-colored attack shrimp. Of the real Winnie the Pooh. Of octopuses with ear-like fins that live in the deepest parts of the ocean. Of enormous birds wreaking havoc. Of a monkey that uses its fingers for echolocation. Of a rude parrot. If you want to be informed, read on.

Places have their own stories to share. A tiny island full of rabbits. A park named after a whale. A triangle in the sea that may make ships and aircraft disappear. A scorching valley where rocks move. If you want to learn of new places to go, read on.

And then there's the truly random stuff. A vanishing room. A sickness that forces its victims to dance. A flood of molasses. A journey across the sea of small, plastic toys going on for miles and decades. If you want to be surprised, read on.

Here you'll find humor, drama, and oddity. Here you'll find people being foolish and wise, wicked and kind. Here you'll travel through time and space, through experiences and knowledge to learn about this world we live in. Here you'll meet charming and intense creatures. Read on to see that absurdity covers this earth like icing on a cupcake.

A FORTUNATE MISFORTUNE

Alexander sighed as he closed and locked the door. Things were going well for him at Kortright and Cruger's trading firm. When Mr. Cruger got sick last year, he'd sailed away from the West Indies, leaving Alexander in charge. People liked him. They thought he was doing a good job. But Alexander was tired of tallying up pounds of flour and counting out bills for traders. As he wiped the fish smell from his hands, he couldn't help but wish that he could be doing something more important.

Rain began to fall, and a wind started up as he plodded home, pushing him forward. He put his head down. There must be a storm coming. He hoped Sarah had remembered to latch his window, so his books didn't get wet.

As he opened the door, Mrs. Stevens called to him. "Alexander! Thank goodness you're finally home. Go and get me some more wood for the fire."

"It's good to see you too, Mrs. Stevens."

"What?"

"Never mind."

Alexander trudged back out into the rain and picked up a stack of drenched firewood.

"Well, this is no good as wet as it is!" Mrs. Stevens complained.

"It's raining outside," Alexander said. "I don't know how you expect dry wood when it's storming."

"None of your sass, young man!" She waved her spoon at him.

"Anna," Mr. Stevens didn't look up from his stack of papers, "leave the boy be."

The wind howled in a way that made all of them look to the window.

"My, it's going to be a bit of a guster, I think," Mrs. Stevens said.

"Look at those trees," Sarah said, pressing her nose against the glass.

The trees were bent like grass in a breeze, and as they watched, one of them broke, crashing into a house. Sarah screamed. A huge branch blew past their window. The wind's howl grew louder and louder.

"This is more than a guster," Mr. Stevens whispered. "This is a hurricane."

Another branch hit the window, cracking the glass. Mrs. Stevens screamed with Sarah this time.

They all sat there, dumbstruck, watching the storm. The fire died out, and their dinner sat forgotten over the embers. Clash upon clash of lightning lit the sky. Houses tumbled to the ground. People screamed. Alexander stared out the cracked window, listening to the groaning wind and wondering if their house was strong enough to stay standing.

After what seemed like years, the air was suddenly still. After waiting several minutes, Alexander and Mr. Stevens lit the lantern and ventured outside. Everything was eerily still, but the air was still hot and humid as it often is before a storm, not after one. They looked around the house and found it nearly undamaged.

The cellar was blocked by the remnants of a roof, and as the two of them tried to pull it free, the wind began again, first a little, then all at once it was roaring, and rain poured over them. They rushed back inside to wait through yet another eternity of screams and crashes and fear.

Alexander must have fallen asleep somehow. He awoke to see daylight shining through the cracked window. He rose and opened the door. The daylight allowed him to see clearly what had become of his town of St. Croix.

He saw houses laid flat. He saw people lying on the ground, injured, while their loved ones tried to attend to them without anywhere to shelter them or any bed to lay them in. He saw a town that looked like a giant had stomped it down in a fit of rage.

Alexander watched his town try to pick up and put itself back together. About a week later, he wrote a letter to his father:

"I take up my pen just to give you an imperfect account of one of the most dreadful Hurricanes that memory or any records whatever can trace."

The letter was published in the newspaper, and the people of the island were astonished at Alexander's skill with words. They wanted to help this young boy realize his talent.

They sent Alexander to New York to receive an education. Alexander Hamilton went to New York in 1772. He fought in the Revolutionary War, became the first Secretary of the Treasury under George Washington, and founded the financial system that the United States of America still uses today. All because he wrote a really good letter about the hurricane that destroyed his town.

THE ONLY IMMORTAL CREATURE

"Have you noticed Andre isn't doing well?" Jasmine asked her fellow jellyfish, Dmitri. "I haven't seen him move in days."

"Oh yeah," said Dmitri, "he ran into the reef yesterday. Squished about five of his tentacles. He went back to being a polyp."

Jasmine sighed. "I wish all our friends would quit becoming polyps. They never have anything to say when they're polyps, and they never want to go anywhere."

"Well," said Dmitri, "they can't really, being stuck to the floor and all."

Jasmine glared at him. "I swear, I think I might need to become a polyp soon, too, so I can escape this boredom."

"You're pretty young, aren't you?"

"I'm a year old. I've been a polyp five whole times."

Dmitri laughed. "Wait until you've done it 500 times. You'll have a little more patience."

In the 1980s, Christian Sommer and Giorgio Bavestrello were studying a group of tiny jellyfish with the scientific name *Turritopsis dohrnii*. It seems they got a little lax in taking care of the jellyfish but, rather than dying, the creatures sunk to the bottom of their tank and seemed to turn into tiny blobs. They retracted their tentacles and shrunk in size. There, they rested for a time.

As the scientists continued to observe them, they realized that the jellyfish had gone back to a former stage in their life cycle, the polyp stage. They, in essence, had gotten younger. Rather than starving to death, *Turritopsis dohrnii* can rejuvenate their bodies by becoming polyps again. They then grow to become full sized medusas, which is the adult stage for a jellyfish.

Some have compared the process to a butterfly, instead of dying, returning to a cocoon and coming back out of it having become a caterpillar again. The jellyfish received the nickname "the immortal jellyfish."

These jellyfish are tiny, about the size of your pinky fingernail. The process in which they revert to their younger life stage is called transdifferentiation, which is the changing of a cell into an entirely different cell. This process is quite rare and Scientists are fascinated by it since they hope to be able to develop the process for human cells, which would allow for amazing new medical opportunities.

The scientists who are studying *Turritopsis dohrnii* have discovered no end to their cycle of growing to adulthood then shrinking back down into polyps when they are starving or injured.

A Japanese scientist named Shin Kubota has been studying these jellyfish since the 1990s, and he saw a group of them transform from medusas to polyps as many as ten times in a two-year span.

It is worth noting though that no one has been able to see this happening outside of laboratory settings, perhaps because it's so hard to see these creatures in the world. It's a little hard to spot a creature in the ocean that's about the size of a garden pea and see-through. It's much easier to observe them in laboratory settings.

Scientists believe these jellyfish first came from the Mediterranean Sea, but they can now be found in oceans across the world. Some think that they ride around by attaching themselves to the sides of ships. And hey, if you're immortal, it's not too hard to get to difficult places.

Turritopsis dohrnii are not completely invincible. Like other tiny creatures, they are always in danger of being eaten by larger creatures. They also can develop infections that kill them. They can only live forever in safe places.

"Look out!" Jasmine cried, diving deep into the water. She looked back up to see the penguin swimming away, gulping contentedly. She didn't see Dmitri. As she swam, looking after the bird, something rammed her up from behind.

"Watch it," the krill said, swimming away.

Jasmine rubbed her tentacles and realized that several were damaged. She sighed. She slowly sank to the ocean floor, pulling her tentacles inside her slowly, shrinking and shrinking until she was even smaller than before, a tiny Jell-O sack on the bottom of the ocean. She rested. She changed once more into a polyp.

TAKE AN ORANGE FOR THE TEAM

"Papa, is it going to start soon?" the little dark-haired girl asks her father, bending down to shout into his ear from her place atop his shoulders.

"Yes, Gianna," he says. "Wait only a bit longer, and it'll begin."

Though their heads are right next to each other, they have to shout to make themselves heard. The crowd around them is massive. Gianna wouldn't be able to see anything at all if she weren't on her father's shoulders. She sits up again and adjusts her red hat.

A rattling is heard down the street. Gianna peers down it, and sees the cart on its way toward them, laden with figures wearing black helmets and black shoulder pads.

"They're almost here!" Gianna squeals. "Can I have your phone, Papa? Can you hand it to me so I can take pictures?"

"I'm not giving you my phone right now, Gianna."

"But Papa, imagine the amazing pictures I'll get! I can see everything from up here!"

"Imagine the damage a stray missile could do to my phone. It's staying in my back pocket, thank you very much."

Gianna groans and then forgets all about it. The cart is completely surrounded by people wearing blue and red jerseys. A cry goes out. Oranges begin to fly.

The people on the ground pelt those on the cart with oranges, throwing them as hard as they possibly can. Juice splatters, pulp flies. Those on the cart gather up the oranges that have been chucked at them, and they begin hurling them back at their attackers. Gianna watches an orange make spectacular contact with a woman's left eye.

"Eesh," she said, "that's going to leave a mark." She sees a man with a bloody nose. "You know, Papa, I'm not sorry that we only watch the Battle of the Oranges."

"Me neither, Gianna," her father said. "Me neither."

The Battle of the Oranges takes place every year in Ivrea, Italy as a part of the Carnival of Ivrea. It happens on the three days leading up to Ash Wednesday, and it's the largest organized food fight in Italy and the surrounding countries. It was established in 1808.

Legend has it that the battle commemorates the overthrow of a wicked tyrant in Medieval times. Apparently, the evil ruler attempted to kidnap a young woman named Violetta on her wedding night. Violetta, after she'd been taken into his house, did not obediently do as she was told. Instead, she cut off his head. The residents of the city then gathered to burn the tyrant's castle down.

In the battle, the armored people on the carts represent the tyrant's army, and the people on the ground represent the common people who defeated the monarch. How the ammo came to be represented by oranges is a bit of a mystery, especially since they're not native to Italy and have to be imported from Sicily.

The battle is an enormous affair and has taken place every year except for during World Wars I and II and during the COVID-19 pandemic. It happened again in 2023 with great success, bringing in record numbers of orange-throwers and spectators.

People who want to beam each other with oranges pay both for their uniforms and the opportunity to be on a team. And there are teams. The "commoners" on the ground are divided into nine teams, and you better know who you're cheering for. It seems that in Ivrea your orange-throwing team ought to have as much of your respect and loyalty as your favorite sports team.

If you're worried about the waste of all the poor oranges, they use fruits that are castoffs which couldn't be sold commercially anyway. Farmers get paid for the 600 tonnes (like tons but a bit heavier) of oranges that are thrown during the battle. When it's all over, the crushed fruit and pulp are carted away to be made into compost and energy.

The shenanigans are buckets of fun, but there is also a bit of danger involved. An orange thrown with all one's force can do some damage.

Though the organizers of the event claim that no one has ever been seriously injured, first aid stations are set up along the road, and it's not uncommon to see blood and bruises blossoming from the citrus bombs. Those who ride the carts typically only do it for one of the three days since they would probably get injured if they tried to do it for all three days.

"Duck!" A stray orange collides with Gianna's shoulder.

"Ow!" she said. "Well, maybe you were smart to keep your phone in your pocket, Papa."

"You think?" he says with a laugh.

The bell rang. Michael jumped up from his desk and beelined for the door, disappearing through it before anyone else had even stood. He sprinted down the hallway, heading for the gym doors and the bulletin board hanging next to them. He'd been checking the board after every class, though Coach Herring had told them the results wouldn't be posted until the end of school. Every time, he'd run to them to see if the lists were up. Every time he'd been disappointed. Until now.

Michael didn't even look at the lower list. His eyes fixed on the top paper, which read "Varsity Basketball!" at its head. He scanned it quickly at first, looking for his own name to jump out at him. He didn't see it. He looked over the list again, this time reading each name carefully. His was not there. He stood there, stunned.

"All right!" a voice said behind him. A hand clapped on his shoulder. "I made it!" Michael turned to see Leroy standing there. "I made varsity, Mike! Sophomores never make varsity!"

Michael didn't say anything to his friend. He turned back to the list, finally looking at the bottom sheet. There was his name at the top. Michael turned away and waded through the crowd of basketball players trying to get a look at the board.

"Hey Mike, did you make it?"

"Mike, did you see my name?"

He didn't answer any of them. He walked back to his locker, shoved his books in his bag, and started home. It was a crisp autumn day. The sky boasted its depth and blueness, and the birds sang like they wanted to bring back summer for good. Michael heard and saw none of it. He opened the front door to see his younger sister, Roslyn, sitting on the couch, watching some dumb kids cartoon. She turned to him and grinned.

"Hi, Mike. How was your day? Did you hear about your tryout?"

Michael walked past her without saying a word. He slammed the door to his room. It felt good.

He lay across his bed, staring up at the ceiling. How had it happened? He had done well at that tryout. He had played his best. And he was good.

He knew he was good. No one could tell him he wasn't. Coach Herring didn't know what he was talking about. None of them did. They would regret having passed him up.

And they'd passed him up for stupid Leroy too! Leroy was a sophomore just like Michael, and he wasn't a better player. Michael knew why they'd picked Leroy. They'd picked him because Leroy had a good seven inches on Michael. He'd hit his growth spurt last summer, but Michael was only a paltry 5' 10".

There was a knock on the door. Michael didn't say anything. The door opened, and his mother walked in.

"It's polite to answer a knock, you know," she said with a faint smile. She sat on the bed next to him.

"You going to sit up and talk to me?" she asked.

He shrugged, still lying on his back.

"Your sister says maybe you didn't make the team like you were hoping you would."

Michael sat up, but he didn't look at his mother. "Roslyn doesn't know anything about it."

"She said you walked in the room, ignored her question about your tryout, and then slammed your door. She can read between the lines. You didn't make it."

"I didn't make varsity," Michael mumbled.

"Speak up. I can't hear you."

"I didn't make varsity." His voice came out as a croak, and he was mortified to feel tears sliding down his nose. He thrust them away angrily. "I did my best. I put everything I had into that tryout. But they didn't think it was good enough."

"Oh baby," his mother put her arms around him, and he leaned into her.

"I'm sorry. I know you really wanted to play with the older guys. But how many sophomores make varsity anyway?"

"Leroy made it."

She laughed. "Of course, Leroy made it. Leroy's a giant." His mother took his chin in her hand and turned him to face her. He was surprised to see tears on her face as well. "You know what you have to do now, don't you?"

"What?"

"If you really want it, you work hard over the summer. You make yourself so good they'll never even think about cutting you. And maybe you'll grow a little in the meantime too."

Michael nodded, wiping more tears away. "Thanks, Mom."

Michael did work hard. He became the junior varsity team's star player, getting as many as 40 points in a game. He continued to practice throughout the summer, and he also grew four to five inches. He made varsity the next year, and after high school, he was recruited by several colleges. After his junior year at University of North Carolina, Michael Jordan was drafted by the Chicago Bulls. He went on to become, in the opinion of many, the greatest basketball player of all time.

ART OR FUN

Mark placed his canvas on the stand and began mixing his paints. One-year-old Marla watched him in fascination. She continued to watch as he dipped his brush and began spreading paint across the canvas.

"Pretty, Daddy."

"Yeah," he said, not really listening. "Daddy's painting."

"Can I do it?" Marla asked, reaching for his palette.

"No!" he shouted, pulling it back from her. "Marla, these are Daddy's paints. I don't want you to make a big mess with them." He wished Laura would watch Marla. He wanted to paint undisturbed. His father had died recently, and he'd been struggling. He hoped that painting might be a good way to express these emotions. But how was he supposed to express his emotions with a toddler grabbing at his paints?

"Can I paint?" Marla asked again.

Mark sighed. He grabbed a sketchpad that was lying around. He got a paper plate and squeezed a few paints on it. He got a brush. He set them on the table and handed Marla the brush.

He pointed back to his canvas. "Those are Daddy's paints." He pointed to the materials on the table. "These are Marla's paints. You use these."

Marla wasn't even looking at him anymore. She'd already dipped the brush in the paint and was smearing it across the sketchpad.

"Good girl," he said, and went back to his painting.

Marla painted throughout the next several weeks. Her pictures didn't look like anything really. She filled page after page with vibrant colors.

Marla played with dolls, she laughed with friends, and she played with her new baby brother. But she always enjoyed pulling out her paints again. Her parents bought more when they ran out.

One night, a friend came over for dinner. After the meal, Marla hopped down from her seat and carried on with a painting.

"You let your three-year-old paint?" the man said. "My goodness, I'd be afraid of the mess."

"She pretty much just keeps it on the paper," Laura said. "We're lucky!" They laughed.

"She did all these," Mark said, picking up the old sketchpad which Marla had completely filled.

Their friend looked them over. "You know, these are actually kind of neat."

"They are pretty, aren't they?" Laura asked, looking over his shoulder.

"You know, I've been looking for something to put on the walls of the coffee shop," he said. "Just something to brighten things up. These would be great. And really, they kinda look like professional art. You know, abstract and all that. Would you mind if I borrowed a few?"

Mark looked at Laura, and she shrugged. "Sure," they said.

A little while after their friend hung the pictures, Laura got a call.

"So, how much would you want to sell Marla's painting for?"

"Sell it?" she said blankly.

"I've got a customer who wants to know how much you want for it."

"Well, I didn't really want to sell it," she said.

"I know, I know, but he was bugging me about. I had to call and ask you. Just say some ridiculously high price, and he'll drop it and leave us alone."

Laura grinned. "All right. Tell him it's $250."

"Perfect," he said. "Stay on the phone just to be sure while I go tell him."

Laura waited a minute. He came back on the line.

"Uh, Laura?"

"Yeah?"

"He said he wants to know who to make the check out to."

Laura took a picture of the check. She smiled at how she would tell Marla about it one day, how she'd painted when she was a toddler, and someone had liked her work so much they'd paid her $250 for it. She told Mark about it. They laughed.

Mark picked up the phone the next time.

"Hello?"

"Are you a parent of the little girl who paints?"

He laughed. "Yeah, I suppose so. Marla's art is hanging in one of the coffee shops downtown. What can I do for you?"

"I'm Anthony Brunelli. I am an artist, and I love what your daughter does. She is a genius! Do you have much more of her work?"

Mark stumbled over his words, surprised at the man's enthusiasm. "Uh, yeah. She's filled up a few sketchbooks with it, and I bought her a few canvases for her fourth birthday. She's finished those too."

Brunelli laughed ecstatically. "She's only four! I knew she was young, but really? Four years old? Incredible. Simply incredible. She truly is a prodigy. I own the gallery on State Street, Anthony Brunelli Fine Arts. If you are agreeable, I'd love to do a show of Marla's work."

"Really?"

"Yes. She is very talented. Her work is magnificent, and I would be honored to share it with the public."

"Well, that's awesome!" Mark said. "We just thought she was a kid having fun. You really think she's a genius?"

"Absolutely. A normal child could not do what she does."

"Wow. We just thought she was a kid having fun with paints, you know?"

"It can be hard to recognize talent in the abstract," Brunelli said.

"Well, let me talk with my wife about it, but, as far as I'm concerned, you can schedule the show."

"Excellent!"

"Can I call you tomorrow?"

"Absolutely!"

Marla's work went on display at the Anthony Brunelli Fine Arts gallery, and it was an astounding success. Her paintings went on to sell for thousands and tens of thousands of dollars. A documentary was made about her when she was seven called My Kid Could Paint That. She fell out of the spotlight after that. She's an adult now, and she still paints, but her work is no longer sold as fine art.

In an interview given when she was fifteen, when she was asked if she considers herself a prodigy said, "I don't think of myself in that way at all."

THE GREAT SPAGHETTI CON

Have you ever been tricked on April Fool's Day? Maybe your mom had the "hilarious" idea to tell you that school was canceled, or your grandpa lined up all your shoes to lead you to the bathroom where a big "April Fool's" was written in lipstick on the mirror.

The creativity of gags seems endless. But have you ever been fooled by a major corporation?

A couple of big businesses have made place for themselves in the April Fool's Day Hall of Fame.

In 1985, George Plimpton, a reporter for Sports Illustrated, made up a Mets pitcher who could throw a 165-miles-per-hour fastball.

In 2005, Google put out a fake advertisement for a brain-boosting smart drink "Google Gulp," which was supposed to help the drinker "Quench your thirst for knowledge and achieve maximum optimization of their soon-to-be-grateful cerebral cortex."

However, perhaps the oldest corporate April Fool's joke was put out by the BBC on April 1, 1957.

The short documentary was shown as the closing segment of Panorama, a respected news show of the day.

The scene opened with soothing mandolin music and images of scenic landscapes and budding trees. We are told that we are in Ticino, a region bordering Italy and Switzerland. The camera then transitions from flowering trees to trees with long strands hanging from them. The narrator explains,

"The past winter, one of the mildest in living memory, has had its effect ... Most important of all, it's resulted in an exceptionally heavy spaghetti crop."

A woman appears and begins plucking strands from the tree. The program goes on to talk about spaghetti farms, how the families lay their spaghetti harvest out in the sun to dry, how the uniform length of the noodles is the, "result of many years of patient endeavors by plant breeders," and how the farmers are particularly fortunate that year because of the "disappearance of the spaghetti weevil," which is, of course, is the blight of every serious spaghetti farmer.

The farmers dutifully and carefully place their spaghetti in wicker baskets and then lay them out to dry. The documentary ends with a scene of the happy farmers enjoying large plates of "home-grown spaghetti."

Charles de Jaeger, a cameraman for the station, sparked the documentary. He said he got the idea from an elementary school teacher who had made the statement: "Boy, you're so stupid, you'd believe me if I told you that spaghetti grows on trees."

The station went all out on this production, giving de Jaeger a budget that would be just a little less than $4000 today. He flew to the Ticino region, bought twenty pounds of pasta, and happily filmed his farce.

They got Richard Dimbleby, a respected news anchor to record the voiceover for them, and he did it in the classic, deadpan fashion so typical of the BBC.

How did people respond to this prank? The station's phones started ringing as soon as the program finished airing. They wanted to know more about pasta farming! Many were angry to learn that the whole thing was a hoax. So many people called that the BBC had to issue a statement proclaiming the program to be a hoax:

"The BBC has received a mixed reaction to a spoof documentary broadcast this evening about spaghetti crops in Switzerland. The hoax Panorama program, narrated by distinguished broadcaster Richard Dimbleby, featured a family from Ticino in Switzerland carrying out their annual spaghetti harvest.

It showed women carefully plucking strands of spaghetti from a tree and laying them in the sun to dry. But some viewers failed to see the funny side of the broadcast and criticized the BBC for airing the item on what is supposed to be a serious factual program. Others, however, were so intrigued they wanted to find out where they could purchase their very own spaghetti bush."

THE UGLIEST MERMAID

The ship rocked, spilling a bit of soup on the table and nearly overturning the lantern. The sailors sighed. They had been away from home for five months. They missed their families, their homes. They missed sleeping in beds instead of hammocks. They missed their wives. They missed eating in rooms that didn't move and spill their dinner.

"Do you think we might head back to Spain soon?" one asked the group. "We've been bouncing from island to island for weeks now, and we haven't found much gold or silver or gems or any of the other stuff Columbus was looking for."

"And, if we haven't found it by now," said his mate with a tap on his nose, "why would we think we'd be finding it in the future? Best to call it a day and sail back."

"Yeah," said yet another. "We found the land, didn't we? We made it to the East Indies. Isn't that the main thing we were looking for?"

The group murmured in agreement.

The cabin boy rushed down the stairs into the room. "Come on, men! You've got to see this!"

The sailors raised their eyebrows. Who trusted a cabin boy? The lad had been excited the first time they lost sight of land.

"Columbus has spotted some mermaids!" the boy shouted.

Benches were thrown back as the men scrambled to get to the stairs.

"Do you believe in mermaids?" one asked another.

"After five months at sea," his mate answered him, "I believe in anything that could be mistaken for a beautiful woman."

They rushed to surround Columbus, who stood against the guard rail on the starboard side, a telescope pressed against his eye.

"You know, I really thought they'd be more attractive than that," he muttered. The men clamored to have a look for themselves. "Hold on," he said. "I'm not quite finished."

"You say they're not very attractive?" asked one of the men.

"I think they'd be just about pretty enough for the likes of you, Private Rico."

The men laughed.

"There, you fellows have a turn," Columbus said, turning his back on the sea and handing over his telescope. The men scrambled for it, each of them looking for mere seconds before it was pulled from his hands to be used by another.

"Those are mermaids?"

"They're awful large women, aren't they?"

"Which end is the head?"

"I don't know what that is, but there's no way it's a mermaid."

"Why not?"

"That looks nothing like a woman!"

"Well, it kind of does. If you look at it the right way."

"Maybe that part is the head?"

The men looked and looked, for a moment forgetting their homesickness while caught up in the excitement of a mermaid sighting.

When Christopher Columbus sailed from Spain across the Atlantic in search of a new trade route to Asia, he kept a journal. In that journal, Columbus recorded, only a few days before the Niña, Pinta, and Santa Maria set sail for their return journey, a mermaid sighting.

Historian Bartolome de las Casas wrote this about it: "When the Admiral [Columbus] went to the Rio del Oro, he saw three mermaids that rose well out of the sea; but they are not so beautiful as they are painted, though to some extent they have the form of a human face. The Admiral says that he had seen some, at other times, in Guinea ..."

Did Christopher Columbus actually see mermaids? Indeed, did he see them multiple times? Modern historians don't think so. In fact, they think Columbus mistook manatees for mermaids.

How could a person mistake these massive, blubbery mammals for creatures that were half-woman? Some theorize that, since heavier women were considered more attractive back then, perhaps this made the mistake easier to make. The other theory, which is considerably more likely, is that the sailors missed being around ladies so much that they could imagine just about anything that they couldn't see very well was a woman.

Columbus spread a lot of misinformation on his return back to Spain. He told them that he had sailed to Asia, which he hadn't. He dubbed the natives he'd met "Indians," a misnomer that has held on for centuries. And he claimed that mermaids were real and that he had seen them.

AN UNEXPECTED REUNION

Toussaint Charbonneau ushered his young wife into the tavern. He scanned the room. "Over there, Saca. This way." He guided her to a table where two men in suits sat. The men nodded at Charbonneau and his wife as they approached and sat down. She thought wryly of how she'd seen men stand and pull-out chairs for white women. But then, she'd never wanted to be treated like a white woman. She was no flower whose petals might blow free in a gust of wind.

"How lovely to meet you, Mrs. Charbonneau," the younger man said, speaking very loudly and slowly as if she were hard of hearing and understanding. "I am Merriweather Lewis. This is my companion, William Clark."

She nodded at them silently, keeping her eyes down.

"Charmed to meet you," said Clark, also speaking slowly but not so loudly. "How soon shall the baby arrive?"

"Soon," she said, still without looking at them.

The men chortled. "I'm glad to know she speaks French," Lewis said.

"Oh yes, she's a smart one," said her husband. "You never know how good a prize you'll pick up in a game of cards, fellas. I tell you, you never do know."

Clark raised his eyebrows. "You … won your wife in a game of cards?"

Charbonneau cackled. "That's right! But it's a story for another time. Now we've got all our things out front. We're ready to follow you as soon as you say the word."

"Could you have your wife demonstrate for us," Lewis said, "these languages you say she speaks?"

"Can we leave soon?" she said in Hidatsa to her husband. "This tavern is hot."

He laughed yet again. "See there, men? She said she wants to leave because it's hot in here." The men laughed together again. "Now say something in Snake, deary."

"I wish you all would leave me alone," she said in Shoshone. "I need a nap, and this baby keeps kicking me. If we're going to stay with you, let's go and be done with it."

"And I don't have any idea of what she just said," said Charbonneau. They all laughed again and shook hands. Lewis and Clark thought she was perfect.

Sacagawea gave birth to her son, Jean Baptiste, at Lewis and Clark's Fort Mandan that February. The four of them set out with about forty other men down the Missouri River the following April.

The men complained about how hard the journey was, but Sacagawea kept quiet. Though she had to take care of her two-month-old son in addition to helping set up and tear down the camp, cook, clean, and load the boats, she saw no good in whining about it. But she was used to hard work and the complaining of men. She had seen this even when she lived with her people.

Sacagawea made herself useful. She saved priceless supplies that tumbled from her boat during a storm. She gathered roots, plants, and berries to eat or use as medicines. She did all this with as few words as possible.

One day, soon after they started, they met with their first Shoshones, two men riding horses at a distance.

"Are these your kind?" Clark asked Sacagawea. She nodded.

She stepped out from the group and signaled to the horsemen, who had been watching their group. They came closer.

She shouted to them as soon as they might be within earshot.

"Peace to you, brothers."

She shouted it several more times until they heard her and shouted back, "Peace to you, sister."

Then they were there. Her heart beat faster as she saw their dark faces and the beading on their buffalo-hide clothes. These were her people.

"What brings you here, sister," the taller of the men said, "and why with these white men?"

"We come to explore," Sacagawea said. "The white man's government wants to cross the land to get to the big waters in the West. They brought me that I might talk to you for them."

"Tell them we want to buy horses from them!" Lewis called.

Sacagawea told them.

"You must speak to our leader," the taller man said. "He will negotiate the exchange."

Sacagawea nodded and told her companions. They followed the two men back to their village.

Her heart leapt as she saw the teepees rising in front of them. She saw a woman painstakingly sewing beads on a shirt. She saw children helping their mother laying out fish to dry. She saw a group of men sitting in a circle, telling stories and smoking pipes.

"These are your people, little one," she whispered to the child on her back. "Look and see your people."

The men led the Charbonneaus, Lewis, and Clark into a large teepee where another group of men sat smoking.

"Cameahwait," the shorter man said, "we have found a sister traveling with a large group of white men. She says they come in peace and that they wish to buy horses from us."

"Cameahwait," Sacagawea murmured, staring at the tall man who had risen. She could not tear her eyes from him. "Cameahwait," she said more loudly now, "is it you, brother?"

He stared at her now, his brow creased. "Yes, I am Cameahwait. You ... could you be Sacagawea?"

Tears began to roll down her cheeks as she nodded. She rushed to him, gripping him around the waist.

"Little sister," he said tenderly, putting his arms around her. "You have come home after so long."

Sacagawea did travel with Lewis and Clark as an interpreter. She proved herself useful in many ways, helping them navigate, finding food and medicine sources, and helping them appear less threatening to Native American tribes they met along the way. She did reunite with her brother, Cameahwait, on this journey, but she did not stay with him. She traveled all the way to the Pacific and back with Lewis and Clark.

THE MAN WHO MADE FLUSHING FAMOUS

The man opened the door for his young fiancé, and she took his arm after they entered. They looked around the room at the pretty porcelain shining in the sunlight from the front window.

"They are pretty, aren't they?" said the woman, running her hand along the top of one of them. "But still, do you think we can afford this?"

"My young wife deserves the best there is," the man said, pecking her on the cheek.

"I almost wonder," she whispered, "if it would be easy to go on one of these. They look so pretty. It seems a pity to use them for waste."

"Welcome to Edward Crapper and Company," a clerk said, smiling broadly at them. "May I help you?"

"We're just browsing, my man," the gentleman said.

The clerk smiled. "Well, you're browsing in the right place. Prince Albert himself ordered about thirty of our lavatories last week. Nice lot, that. Cedar seats on every one. So, if the crown trusts us, you know you can too."

"Can we ask about the cost," the woman said, glancing at her husband-to-be.

The clerk named a price.

"Oh dear," she sighed. "It seems a waste. I grew up on a farm, you see, and we always used the outhouse without difficulty. Dear, are you certain we need one of these fancy flushing toilets?"

The clerk smiled. "They aren't as cheap as a loaf of bread, I'll say, but they do last quite a bit longer. And so convenient to have them right there in the house with you!

And with Mr. Crapper's new U-Bend installments, it's nearly impossible to jam them. And you'll never have to worry about the stench that comes from an outhouse with these either."

The couple continued to look around, dreaming of living in a house with an indoor bathroom and a toilet that actually flushed.

Thomas Crapper (yes, that is his real name) did not invent the flushing toilet. It was first patented by Alexander Cumming in 1775. Crapper was, however, the first lavatory salesman to create a showroom for his toilets. He may not have invented flushers, but he did make them a great deal more popular than they'd ever been before.

Crapper apprenticed as a plumber under his brother George and then worked as a general plumber for three years. He set up his own plumbing business in 1861. He didn't just sell toilets, but he also improved them. We can thank him both for the U-bend in toilets, which was a significant upgrade from the S-bend which existed before, which was liable both to clog and dry out. He also invented the floating ballcock, that ball that sits on top of the water in many toilets and keeps them from overflowing.

Crapper did take orders from royalty, and his business is still around today. The use of the word "crap" to mean excrement did not come from Crapper, though there is a story about U.S. military men seeing the word "crapper" on the toilet and starting to say things like "I'm going to the crapper." This story is a legend at best.

The word crap is much older than Mr. Crapper, going back to Middle English, most likely being a combination of the Dutch word "krappen" (to pluck off, cut off, or separate) and the old French word "crappe" (siftings, waste, or rejected matter). This word was originally used to refer to husks left after harvest, weeds, or other garbage. The word was first used to refer to poop in 1846, ten years after Crapper's birth, when people used the words "crapping ken" to refer to a toilet. Perhaps the term should come back to popularity.

POLL THE PARROT SAYS GOOD-BYE

"It's hard to imagine it," the woman said as she, her husband, and their son walked down the dirt road. "It's hard to imagine that a man as important as that could actually die."

Her husband laughed. "Everyone dies, Amanda."

"Well, yes, I know," she said. "But still, it's hard to imagine him, President Andrew Jackson, dead."

They weren't the only ones walking the road to the Hermitage, Jackson's Tennessee home, that day. Thousands flocked to pay their respects. All of them in their funeral black had turned the road into a great, dark, slow-flowing river.

"I know just what you mean," said a young woman walking nearby. "With how he fought all those battles, led our country, and even when that man tried to shoot him, what did President Jackson do? He just picked up his walking stick and whacked him a good one. Goodness, it just seems like it's hard for a man like that to die."

"He's been a strong one, that's certain," said Amanda's husband, "but no one escapes death in the end."

The little boy tugged on Amanda's sleeve. "Will we get to see the body, Mama?"

"Joshua! What a horrid thing to think about!"

"Well Mama, it's just that I've never seen a real live body before."

"The body won't be live, son," said his father.

They could see the house now, and it was already surrounded by people. They waited a long time to be able to go in. Joshua pulled a ball from his pocket, throwing it up and catching it again and again. His mother made him quit when he missed and the ball hit a nearby elderly woman.

Slowly, they made their way up the steps and into the house. Slowly, they walked toward the casket.

Suddenly, a great racket was heard. A shrill shrieking sounded forth, and Joshua had to cover his ears.

39

Everyone looked around for the source of the noise. A large red parrot sat on a perch near the center of the house. The bird flapped its wings nervously, and it shrieked and shrieked. Some of the noises were just shrill squawks, but many of them were words. They were words that Joshua wasn't allowed to use, amd some of them were words that he'd never even heard before. His mouth fell open in awe.

"Stop it! Stop it, you ridiculous bird!" a man in a black suit said, drawing close to the parrot. The bird only directed its stream of cuss words at the man instead of at the crowd in general.

The man proceeded to pick up the bird stand and carry it out of the house, the crowd parting for him like the Red Sea. Joshua heard the bird's swearing grow fainter and fainter until it was gone.

"Good gracious," said Amanda. "What a horrid bird."

"Well, you can't blame the parrot, Amanda," Joshua's father said. "It only knows what it's been taught."

Amanda stared at him with wide eyes. "Do you think that was President Jackson's bird? Do you think President Jackson would ever use such awful language?"

"Well," Joshua's father laughed, "I'd be a bit surprised if President Jackson didn't have his share of rough language, dear. He was an army man for a great deal of his life. And you know how army men talk."

They were able to see the body soon after that, and Joshua stared into the casket. It almost looked like President Jackson was smiling a little, laughing at the grand display his bird had given to send him off.

President Jackson did own a parrot named Poll. He bought him as a gift for his wife Rachel and became its caretaker after her death. Reverend William Menefee Norment gave this report about what the bird did at Jackson's funeral.

"Before the sermon and while the crowd was gathering, a wicked parrot that was a household pet got excited and commenced swearing so loud and long as to disturb the people and had to be carried from the house."

Norment said the parrot was "excited by the multitude and ... let loose perfect gusts of 'cuss words.'" The onlookers were "horrified at the bird's lack of reverence."

Most conclude that the parrot learned the profanity from Jackson himself. He showed no regret about ripping tens of thousands of Native Americans from their homes and sending them on the Trail of Tears to go live on "Indian Territory." Jackson was a rough man. It would have been odd if Poll were a polite parrot.

HUNTING TO SAVE

"Crikey! What a beauty!"

Millions of viewers loved listening to Steve Irwin shout his catchphrase as he set out to tackle yet another crocodile. Irwin was an Australian zookeeper who also made it his business to travel throughout his country capturing crocodiles that had showed up in dangerous places. Though Irwin literally wrestled these animals, he didn't view them as enemies. He loved them, and couldn't handle them without being constantly astonished by their power and beauty.

Irwin tackled his first crocodile at the tender age of nine. His parents started the Queensland Reptile and Fauna Park, and Steve was nurtured in his love for animals, particularly reptiles. He grew up to inherit management of the park, which he later renamed Australia Zoo.

Irwin was an enthusiastic animal-lover and conservationist. Though he's known as the crocodile hunter, he hunted not to kill but to relocate. His purpose was always to help the creatures as much as he could.

As Irwin put it, "My job, my mission, the reason I've been put onto this planet, is to save wildlife." He thought that by showing the public how awesome the animal kingdom was, people would come to love them. And if they loved animals, they would take steps to protect them. He tried to spread the contagion of his own enthusiasm.

"If you can't excite people about wildlife, how can you convince them to love, cherish, and protect our wildlife and the environment they live in?" Irwin said.

After watching the crocodile hunter wrestling crocs and handling aggressive and venomous snakes, it was easy to believe he was invincible. Indeed, for a while it seemed he thought it himself, making statements like, "I've worked with more dangerous snakes than anyone in the world, and I've never been bitten. It's a gift."

The gift didn't last, though. Irwin was later filmed being bitten by a snake on live TV. His response? He told the camera to zoom in.

It was normal to watch Irwin sustaining minor injuries throughout the course of the show.

Irwin's job was dangerous. He always knew this. Indeed, he talked about how fear helped keep his senses sharp and how he knew he might one day face his death at the claws, teeth, or sting of one of these animals. He didn't seem perturbed at the idea of this, saying, "I have no fear of losing my life—if I have to save a koala or a crocodile or a kangaroo or a snake, mate, I will save it." Though viewers might have thought he'd meet his end in the jaws of a croc, in the end, it was a stingray that led to Steve Irwin's death.

Irwin was in the Great Barrier Reef filming for a documentary. One day the weather was too lousy, so he set out to get some different footage for a show his daughter starred in, Bindi the Jungle Girl. Irwin saw a stingray and tried to follow it to capture it on film. The fish freaked out, stinging Irwin over and over again in a couple of seconds. His team worked hard to save him but it wasn't enough.

It is extremely rare for stingrays to behave this way. They only kill one to two people a year. Crocodiles, on the other hand, kill about 1,000 people per year.

Though Irwin isn't around to show his viewers how to be wildlife warriors anymore, his wife and children carry on running the Australia Zoo and spreading his message of conservationism.

As his son Robert, now a wildlife photographer, said, "I hope in every aspect of my life that I can make him proud … I want to have an even bigger voice to make sure that that message never ever dies. Because he always said, 'I don't care if people remember me, I care if people remember my message.' And I want to make sure that continues."

THE BATH TOY ARMADA

Lightning lit the black sky as the wind howled, fighting to be heard over the crashing waves. The storm tossed the freighter about like it was no more than a dandelion in a spring breeze. An enormous wave rose up and over the side of the ship, washing over the decks with tremendous force.

The containers sitting on the deck were forty feet high and enormously heavy, but they were no match for the waves. Into the sea, twelve of the containers plummeted. Most of them quickly sank to the depths, likely never to be seen again. But one was different, though. One container popped open.

Out into the boiling ocean spewed 28,800 bath toys. Yellow ducks, red beavers, green frogs, and blue turtles were tossed and rolled by the waves. They didn't sink like the rest of the cargo, though. They were made to float. No matter how many times they were pushed under, they popped up again, ready to start an adventure that could last decades.

The next day, they all floated together in the middle of the Pacific Ocean, bobbing peacefully in the after-storm calm. They seemed to be looking at each other asking, where will we go from here? The answer was... Everywhere.

In 1992, this actually happened. The Friendly Floatees, as they were soon named, burst out of a shipping container owned by First Years Inc. during a storm in the pacific, spilling nearly 30,000 bath toys into the ocean.

Scientists have used accidents like this to study ocean currents for a while now. An oceanographer named Curtis Ebbesmeyer hired beachcombers to help him find the toys and started to chart their progress around the world.

The first Friendly Floatees to end their journey washed up on the coast of Alaska at the end of that year, having traveled 2,000 miles. 400 more washed up on Alaska's east coast a bit later.

As they were found, Ebbesmeyer entered their locations into an Ocean Surface Currents Simulation, called OSCAR for short. OSCAR tried to guess where the bath toys would end up next.

OSCAR correctly predicted that the next batch would wash on the shores of Washington state in a few years. Some wandered toward Japan and then back to Alaska. Some headed up to the Arctic, traveling across the ice floes in a few years. When they reached the other side, some broke free of the ice and traveled south again.

In 2003, The First Years began offering a $100 savings bond to anyone who turned in one of the bath toys. OSCAR predicted that the ducks would begin arriving in the southwest shores of the UK, and locals who heard about it awaited their appearance with excitement. By this time, the bath toys were bleached white but still recognizable by the company logo "The First Years" stamped on them. After a journey of fifteen years and 17,000 miles, many were found washed ashore on the UK's western coast between 2003 and 2007. Some continued to travel, being discovered in places like Australia, South America, and South Africa.

The Friendly Floatees have taught scientists a lot about ocean currents, and they've had an impact on culture as well. Eric Carle wrote a children's book about the Friendly Floatees called *10 Little Rubber Ducks*, and Donovan Hohn wrote a whole book called *Moby Duck: The True Story of 28,800 Bath Toys Lost at Sea*.

Some of the Floatees are still out there somewhere. Many are probably still trapped in the Great Pacific Garbage Patch or frozen in the Arctic. Next time you're on an ocean beach, keep your eyes open for a white duck, beaver, turtle, or frog with the words "The First Years" stamped on it. Take a long look and imagine the amazing story it has to tell.

THE REAL WINNIE

Harry Colebourn stepped down from the train car into the White River Station. He yawned and stretched. The journey had been long, and it was far from over.

As he looked around, something small and furry caught his eye. It was no wonder. Before turning soldier, Colebourn had just earned his veterinary license. He loved animals. He had to see what kind this one was. As he drew closer, he saw it was a bear cub on a leash.

"My good man," said Colebourn to the man holding the leash, "what have you got there?"

"It's a cub," said the man. "The friendliest little creature you ever did see. I hunted her ma the other day and finished her off. She'll feed my family for a good while, let me tell you. But when I saw her little cub, well, I couldn't bring myself to leave her. Just look at her. Could you have done it?"

"I should think not," said Colebourn. The fuzzy, black cub was sniffing him, and Colebourn rubbed it around the ears. It crooned with pleasure.

The hunter laughed. "She likes you. Well, I've brought her here to see if someone wants to buy her. Like I said, she's the friendliest little creature. I'm only asking twenty-five dollars for her."

"Twenty-five dollars?"

"That is what I'm asking, sir."

The bear crawled into Colebourn's lap and started licking his face. The young vet laughed. "I'll give you twenty dollars, a solid, friendly handshake, and the knowledge that the bear likes its owner."

The hunter cackled. "Think your handshake is worth a full five dollars, do you? And the bear liking you doesn't mean a thing. I told you, she's as friendly as a mosquito."

The train whistle blew, and men started pouring back onto the train. The hunter looked over and frowned.

"All these young fellows turning soldier and heading across the world to fight the Germans. What a sorry business it is."

"I'm going with them," Colebourn said.

"Are you then, lad?"

"Yes, sir. Heading to Quebec for training right this moment."

The hunter took Colebourn's hand in both of his. "Well then, a handshake with a brave soldier. That handshake is worth five dollars. Bless you for your service, lad."

"Thank you, sir."

"And you take good care of this cub. Don't make her fight the Germans. She's too friendly for that."

"Of course not, sir. Thank you."

The money changed hands, and Colebourn headed back onto his train. The bear went with Colebourn to training camp and then across the sea to England. He named her Winnipeg after his hometown and called her Winnie for short. Colebourn trained her, giving her treats of apples and condensed milk. She was popular with the men and became something of a mascot for his regiment.

Eventually, Colebourn had to head off for war, and he couldn't take Winnie with him. He decided to leave her at the London Zoo. Winnie became an instant success. She was so friendly that children even rode on her back and fed her by hand.

One child in particular came to adore Winnie. He constantly begged his father to take him to the London Zoo to see her. His name was Christopher Robin Milne. He renamed his teddy bear, formerly called Edward, after her. His father began to write books about the adventures of Christopher's stuffed animals, and thus the Winnie the Pooh books were born.

Colebourn returned to see Winnie after World War I ended, but he couldn't bring himself to steal her from all the London children who loved her so.

He headed back to Canada without her. Winnie became famous through A. A. Milne's children's stories, and when she passed away at twenty years old, there was news of it around the world. There is a statue of her in the London Zoo and another in the Assiniboine Park Zoo in her namesake town of Winnipeg.

RABBITS AND MORE RABBITS

Goro sat up, stretching his ears as high as they would go.

"Anzu?"

The rabbit, who had been snoring contently next to him, groaned. "Goro, I was napping. You know how important naps are to me."

"But Anzu, I think someone's coming!"

"So what?" Anzu nestled back into the grass, hoping Goro would leave her alone so she could go back to sleep.

"Maybe they'll come over here! Maybe they'll have food! Maybe they'll refill our water pan!"

"Maybe. If they do, let me know. But there are too many humans around here. I'm not going to do a song and dance every time I see one."

Okunoshima, or Rabbit Island, in Japan is currently home to more than 900 rabbits. Guests come from all over the world to see the stunning views and the amazing crowds of rabbits. The bunnies are so used to tourists that its quite normal for them to get very close to visitors and even chase them.

Where did all the rabbits come from? They're European rabbits, so you can be sure they're not native. Okunoshima used to be home to a secret military plant after World War I and during World War II. The scientists used rabbits in their lab for experiments. Some people think the rabbits are descendants of these rabbits, but United States troops claimed that when they liberated the island, they didn't leave any rabbits behind. It's hard to know, though. Some could have escaped and populated the island.

It's more commonly believed that students on a school field trip set eight rabbits free on the island.

With no natural predators and plenty of food and water, the rabbits did what rabbits do best: made more rabbits.

The population now poses a bit of a problem for the bunnies. Okunoshima doesn't have enough food and water to keep them all in good health. The people running the attraction have set out water pans and encourage patrons to refill them. The rabbits also depend on food from tourists.

If you want to visit Rabbit Island, make sure you know the rules. Don't pick up the rabbits, chase them, feed them human food, leave your leftovers lying on the ground, or take them home. And make sure to refill the rabbits' water pans.

Japan hosts several animal islands that attract tourists. They have a horse island, a deer island, a monkey island, a sheep island, two dolphin islands, and three cat islands. If you want to see a large population of furry creatures, going on an island-hopping vacation in Japan might be just right for you.

A mother and her small son appeared, and Goro hopped all around their feet, staring up into their faces expectantly. The woman smiled and reached into her bag. She handed a cabbage leaf to the little boy. He eagerly bent down and held it out to Goro, who snatched it up. He carried it in triumph back to Anzu.

"See! I told you they would help us!"

She opened one eye to stare at the leaf and sniffed it. She reclosed her eye. "That's cabbage. It'll just upset your stomach."

"But it's food, Anzu! It's food!"

"I'll wait for the people who know things about rabbits and bring us the right kind of food."

"It's not people who are the problem around here," said Goro, "it's rabbits. There are too many rabbits."

"Well, you're part of that problem, Goro."

"I know." Goro hung his ears. "I don't know what to do about that."

Anzu sighed. "Eat your cabbage, and follow the people all you want."

"Yay!" Goro hopped off to chase the little boy.

WATCH OUT FOR THAT WHALE!

"Are they gonna do it soon?" Lila asked her mother.

"I don't know, honey," her mother said. "We've just got to be patient."

"Is it going to blow the whole whale into the sky?" Lila's little brother, Andre, asked.

"Not in one piece," Lila said. "The explosion will break it into little pieces. And then the pieces are supposed to land in the water."

"Wow," Andre said.

"Hopefully, whatever happens, it'll get rid of the stink," said their mother.

They stared at the huge mass lying on the beach. Suddenly, the blast went off, and a brown mushroom of sand shot up into the sky.

"Did it work? Did it work?" Andre asked, jumping up and down.

"I can't see," Lila said. "The sand's still everywhere."

Then they heard what sounded like a heavy rain falling. Pieces of something slimy began to land all around them and on their clothes, on their skin, and in their hair. Lila's mother swore as she grabbed her children's hands and ran them toward their car.

"What is it, Mama?" Andre said. "Why are we running?"

"Don't worry about it, sweetie, just run with me," she said.

"Wait," said Lila, "is this stuff pieces of the whale?! Are these whale guts landing on us? Ew!" She picked up her pace and reached the car before her mother and brother, yanking the door open, jumping inside, and slamming it behind her.

A huge crash sounded nearby. The family looked over to see that a nearby car had been utterly smashed by an enormous piece of the whale carcass.

On November 9, 1970, a forty-five-foot, eight-ton sperm whale washed up dead on a beach in Florence, Oregon. It had been so long since officials had had to deal with a beached whale that they didn't know what to do. They thought about burying it, but they thought it would quickly be uncovered. They considered cutting it up, but no one wanted the job. They thought about burning it, but this would have been extremely difficult.

While they pondered the question, the whale started to rot, spreading a heavy stench throughout the beach. They decided something must be done, and fast.

Engineers from the Oregon State Highway Division were sent to blow up the whale. They thought that, if they set off dynamite beneath it, the carcass would be broken up into small enough pieces that seagulls could clean up the remains. They set up twenty cases of dynamite all on the side of the whale farthest from the ocean with hopes of blowing a large portion of the carcass into the water. Civilians were sent a quarter mile away from the blast for their own safety.

When the dynamite detonated, whale remnants flew incredible distances. One huge chunk did indeed crush a car more than a quarter mile away from the blast. As the reporter sent to cover the story put it, "The blast blasted blubber beyond all believable bounds." Whale remnants splattered down on the citizens of Florence while a huge portion of the whale remained on the beach, untouched by the blast. Workers had to return to remove it the next day.

The town wasn't damaged in any significant way. The man who reported on the explosion, Paul Linnman, became famous as the guy who reported on the exploding whale. He said he gets asked about the whale all the time. "I was asked about it virtually every day" Linnman said.

Though the whale removal was a bit of a catastrophe, Florence now claims to be home to the famous event with pride. In 2020, they opened a park named "Exploding Whale Memorial Park" to mark the 50th anniversary of the event. The park overlooks the beach. Hopefully, it never happens again.

Isabella marched through the fields like a soldier. She would tell her old master what was what. She simply could not believe they had done this. They had taken him. They had taken her little Peter, and they had sold him down South.

She had known that he'd been sold before she'd left her master. She'd watched him ride away in the buggy, tears streaming down her face as he looked back at her, not daring to raise his voice and call for her. She'd watched that little face, barely five years old, disappear over the hill.

Her old master, Mr. Dumont, had tried to be courteous. He'd told her in advance that he was selling her son.

"Now Bell," he'd said, "you know you have five children. That's quite a lot, isn't it. And you know that they're really my children by rights. But I'll take care of them for you. I'll send Peter to a good, nice home. I'll send him where he'll be treated kindly, just as you have been. I'll sell him to Dr. Gedney. You know he's a nice man. You know that a slave in a doctor's house has it easy. And Dr. Gedney is in town quite close by. He'll be so close to you. And he'll still be freed at twenty-one as the law says."

And she'd nodded and said nothing. What could she say? He was her son, but he was Mr. Dumont's property. So, she'd watched him go without a word.

But now she knew that Peter hadn't stayed with Dr. Gedney. Gedney had decided Peter was too small to help him, and he'd passed him off to a brother who'd passed him off to a brother-in-law in Alabama.

Alabama. Down South. Where the big plantations were. Where slaves were not just owned but, in many places, treated worse than livestock. Her sweet, little Peter. She couldn't stand it.

She knocked at the front door with a fist full of wrath. Mrs. Dumont opened it.

"You've let them sell Peter down South," Isabella said without preamble, her voice full of quiet fury.

"You've broken the law and let them sell my poor little Peter down there so far away from me and from all he's known to those wicked men who will treat him God knows how horribly. How could you, Mrs. Dumont? How could you let them?"

Mrs. Dumont tsked and sighed, saying she was making such a great fuss.

Isabella looked at her with those cold, dark eyes. "I'll have my child again," she said quietly.

Mrs. Dumont laughed in her face. Isabella left.

She went to Dr. Gedney's house. She talked with his mother, and Mrs. Gedney laughed at her too. Isabella didn't know where to turn or what to do. She prayed and asked God for help.

A few days later, a man who'd heard about Peter told her she must go to the Quakers.

"They've heard about how your son was sold, and they too are greatly distressed about it. Go to them. They'll help you."

Isabella went to the Quakers.

"You must understand, Isabella," a Quaker woman said, "that they haven't just taken your son, but they've illegally sold him out of the state. They can't do that. You must complain to the grand jury. They can force the slave owners to send your son back to you."

The Quakers took Isabella to the courthouse in Kingston, and she marched straight in. She gave her complaint to the first man she saw who looked important, but he told her she must go upstairs to find the grand jury.

She struggled up the stairs through crowds of people and, once again, spoke to the most important-looking man she saw.

He told her he was not the grand jury either and pointed her to where they were sitting. She strode up to them and, once again, began to make her complaint.

The men swore her in on the Bible and had her state her case. Having heard it, the men gave her a writ and told her to give it to her town constable. He would serve it to the man who'd taken her son, Solomon Gedney. Isabella promptly trotted home to do just that.

The constable delivered the notice to Solomon Gedney, and he went to Kingston to await his trial some months in the future. This news terrified Isabella. She didn't know if her son would still be in the same place in several months. She was so bothered that she went about town talking to everyone about her troubles.

One man she spoke to told her, "You must go to Lawyer Demain. He'll help you, I'm sure."

Without a pause, Isabella went to Lawyer Demain's house and told him her situation.

"Get me five dollars," he told her, "and I'll have your son for you in twenty-four hours."

"I don't have any money," she told him.

"Go to those Quakers you told me about," he said, "and get the money from them."

She trotted off the eight or nine miles to see the Quakers, and they gave her the money. She returned and handed Lawyer Demain the money.

"Twenty-four hours," he told her, "and I'll have your son for you."

And the next day, Isabella, after having bothered every authority figure she could find, reunited with her little Peter and took him home for good.

Isabella Van Wagenen was perhaps the first black woman to win a court case against a white man. Her sheer courage and stubbornness won her son back. Several years later, she changed her name to Sojourner Truth.

THE MYSTERY OF THE DISAPPEARED ROOM

Eva stared around the room in wonder. It glittered and shone. Everything was gold and gleaming. Moldings of fat baby cherubs and solemn women stared down at her. Jewels glimmered everywhere. Paintings and golden gilding covered the walls. Candles glowed, casting more yellow light on the warmly colored walls. This place seemed simply too rich to be allowed.

"It's not the real room, though," her brother said from behind her.

"How can a room not be real," Eva asked, turning to face him. "We're standing in it right now."

"But it's not the actual Amber Room," her brother said. "The real one is missing."

"Missing?" Eva was actually laughing at him now. "What are you even saying, Ivan? How can a room go missing?"

Ivan paused. "Well, I'm not really sure how they moved it. But they did. And then, it got lost."

"You're making this up," Eva said.

"No, I'm not! Mom! Tell Eva that this room isn't the real one, that they lost the real one!"

Their mother crossed from the room where she'd been studying the sculpture of a horse and rider. "What's that, Ivan?"

"Tell Eva that this room isn't real!"

Their mother smiled. "Well, it's not fake, Ivan."

"See!" Eva said.

Ivan looked close to tears. "But we learned about it in school, and they said the real Amber Room was lost."

"It was," their mother said.

"What?" Eva cried.

"It was lost," their mother said, "but that doesn't mean this room isn't real. All the materials are real. I suppose most of the paintings are prints, not originals, but still, it's all real gold and amber and jewels. But you are right, Ivan, that it's not the original Amber Room. The first Amber Room, the gift from Frederich I, king of Prussia, to Peter the Great, king of Russia in the 1700s, was lost."

"How can you lose a room?" Eva repeated.

"Well," said her mother with a smile, "that's a bit of a story."

The Amber Room, lined with amber, which is golden-colored fossilized tree sap, was first finished in 1701 in Prussia during the reign of Frederich I. Peter the Great, king of Russia, admired it on a visit. Wanting to strengthen military ties between the two countries, Frederich I gave Peter the Amber Room as a gift. The room was constructed with large panels which could be removed from the walls, so they took the panels down and shipped them to Russia. There they happily decorated Catherine Palace for more than two-hundred years.

When Germany invaded Russia during World War II, valuable artwork was moved away from the battle front. They tried to move the room, but the amber had become brittle over the years and couldn't be moved without crumbling. They decided to cover it with wallpaper and hope the Germans wouldn't notice. They did notice though, and they disassembled it and took it to Königsberg's Castle Museum.

As the war neared its end and the German front was pushed back, Hitler ordered valuables to be moved away from the front. But the Allies were too quick, and many of the treasures were left behind.

As Allies advanced, the Royal Air Force bombed Königsberg, and the Soviet Army (which was largely Russian, ironically) did even more damage to the castle. Official reports said that the Amber Room was destroyed in these attacks.

However, there's much mystery surrounding the disappearance of the room.

There were many reports that it was loaded onto a ship in 1945, but the ship was quickly sunk by a Soviet sub. The room was not found in the wreckage. In 1997, part of one of the room's mosaics was found in a German family's house.

They were descendants of a soldier, who said he stole it when he helped move the room. There were other reports of sightings, but no one ever found it. Some believe it may still be contained in an underground vault beneath Königsberg Castle.

The Soviet government ordered a reconstruction of the Amber Room in 1979. It took twenty-four years to finish, and it was dedicated by Russian President Vladimir Putin and German Chancellor Gerhard Schröder at the 300th anniversary of the city of St. Petersburg.

"And here we are now," said their mother.

"Do you think it was really destroyed?" Eva asked.

"Who knows?" her mother said.

"I don't think so," said Ivan. "I bet it's buried under the castle. Maybe I'll go dig it up someday and become rich and famous. But see, I told you this one wasn't real."

"It may not be the original Amber Room," their mother said, "but I'd say something this beautiful has to be real."

Looking at the shining walls and gleaming statues, the children couldn't argue with that.

THE ULTIMATE DANCE OFF

Staring into the sky, she lifted her skirts and stepped into the square. She began to sway and step, doing a slow dance. Her pace escalated gradually until she was enthusiastically jigging all about. People stared on, surprised at this sudden display of vigor. Frau Troffea was normally such a respectable woman, and here she was, kicking up her heels, hair beginning to fall from her bun, sweat dripping down her face.

"What's happened, Frau Troffea?" the baker called. "What's got you so excited?"

"I-I don't know," Frau Troffea panted. "I can't seem to stop!"

And she didn't stop. Her fellow townspeople in the lovely city of Strasbourg looked on as she kept dancing for nearly an entire week. Her feet were bruised, her hair loose, the bottom of her skirt caked with dirt. Occasionally, she fell to the ground in exhaustion, but, on awakening, she resumed her dancing without delay.

"It's the devil," the seamstress said. "Say a prayer for her."

"It's a sickness," the blacksmith said. "Keep your distance."

His words proved an omen, for soon others began to join Frau Troffea. Dancing without reason, without, it seemed, the ability to stop. The crowd grew and grew until there were hundreds of people dancing uncontrollably.

"It's demons!" some cried.

"It's a plague!" cried others.

The doctors said, "Their blood is too hot. Let them dance. Let them get it out of their systems."

The authorities obliged. They played music for the dancers. They built them a stage in the middle of town. However, this didn't seem to help the people stop.

They continued dancing.

Finally, the religious leaders got involved.

"This is the work of Satan," they said.

"We must take the dancers up the mountain. We must pray for their forgiveness and their freedom from this curse."

They led the dancing people up the mountain to a shrine up Saint Vitus.

"Put the holy shoes on their feet," the priest said.

Red wooden shoes with crosses painted on the tops and soles were put on the feet of the dancers. The priests burned incense, filling the air with its sweet smell. They put crosses in the dancers' hands. They prayed in Latin.

A priest raised his hands. "You are cleansed, children. Saint Vitus has forgiven you! Stop your dancing!"

Gradually, the dancers' feet stilled. Their hands fell to their sides. They slumped to the ground in relief. The plague was over.

Such a plague did in fact take place in the city of Strasbourg, France in the year 1518. The dancing broke out seemingly without reason or warning. It's said that around 400 people were involved, and the doctors did indeed encourage them to cool their "hot blood" by continuing to dance. A number of people did collapse from exhaustion, though there's a dispute about how many.

This isn't the only dancing plague in the historical record. Apparently, others reportedly took place in Switzerland, France, Germany, and Holland. This plague is the last on the historical record.

What caused these people to dance? At the time, people blamed demons and, like the doctors said, hot blood. Now, modern scientists offer several theories. Some think that because of the stressful times people in the town were facing, they developed a mass hysteria that resulted in their continuous dancing.

Some believe that, in a time where it was common to believe in demons and curses, it was easier for the people to convince themselves that they were suffering from such a curse; in short, it was all in their heads. Some still believe that it was, in fact, God's judgment on these people for some reason.

Regardless, we can be glad that such plagues don't happen nowadays.

They stared at the sensor, eyes glued, breaths quiet. Not a word was spoken. The needle ticked up and down on the reader, registering every slightest, tiniest object that touched the photo-electric cell's beam. They watched, observing, wondering what particles were hitting the beam, wondering if, perhaps, it would make contact with particles that may have once belonged to a person now dead. Edison and his friends stared at the reader and wondered if they'd be able to use information from this study to be able to talk to the dead.

Most people think of Thomas Edison as a scientist and inventor. He came out with a record number of patents in his lifetime: 1093. Not all of them were good ideas like the alkaline battery and the talking doll. Some, like his concrete furniture and his ink for the blind, were bad ideas from the start.

Though he did invent some amazing things, like the phonograph, the first device used to record and play back a person's voice. Imagine a world where you not only couldn't record video, but you couldn't record anyone's voice. That was the way things were before Edison's phonograph.

But his most famous invention, ironically, wasn't his invention at all: the light bulb. Edison was a brilliant man, but he was practical. Early in his career, he realized there was greater profit to be found in improving old ideas rather than coming up with new ones. Though lightbulbs had been around for years, they were highly impractical until Edison's. His lasted long enough and were cheap enough to be used by everyday people in their homes. He was largely in the business not of inventing new ideas but of improving old ones.

Though Edison did spend a lot of time fixing other people's old ideas, he did have some of his own. Perhaps the oddest one was one he never had the chance to finish: a phone to talk to the dead.

Edison believed that human beings were made of "myriads and myriads of infinitely small individuals, each in itself a unit of life." He believed these tiny living beings lived forever and functioned in "swarms." According to him, a person is no more than a really big swarm of all these tiny beings.

Since Edison believed little beings couldn't die even if a person dies, he thought that parts of the person were still around after the person died.

He thought the person's personality would be imprinted on these swarms, and if a person could only make contact with the personality swarm, they could talk to someone who was dead. He dreamed of making a phone that would allow people to connect with these swarms, and thus, talk to the dead.

Edison started talking about this invention when he was seventy-three. A lot of people thought he was losing his mind in his old age. They thought he was getting into mysticism when he was supposed to be a scientist. Edison was greatly offended by these accusations. As he said, in regard to his spirit phone, "If this is ever accomplished, it will be accomplished by scientific methods." He saw what he was doing as just another part of his scientific exploration.

Edison never finished his spirit phone. In fact, most people forgot he ever had the idea. Some thought he made up the whole thing as a joke, but a chapter of Edison's last journal includes his ideas for the spirit phone.

This chapter was left out of the original publication of his journal, perhaps because the publishers thought it was too strange and wanted to protect Edison from criticism. He never got so far as to build a prototype, but there was a news article that discussed Edison's research on the phone. According to the article, he gathered a group of scientists in 1920.

It went on to say: "Edison set up a photo-electric cell. A tiny pencil of light, coming from a powerful lamp, bored through the darkness and struck the active surface of this cell, where it was transformed instantly into a feeble electric current. Any object, no matter how thin, transparent, or small, would cause a registration on the cell if it cut through the beam."

Apparently, Edison and the group of scientists stared at the instrument for hours, but they never really gained much information from it. The phone never got finished, and Edison died several years later. Perhaps, if Edison is right, the swarms of his personality are still wandering around, trying to find a way to contact the living so he can finish his invention.

THE FURIOUS RAINBOW WARRIORS

"I'm hungry," said the octopus to no one in particular.

"You're always hungry," said a nearby sea anemone.

"I wasn't talking to you," said the octopus. A crustacean skitters by, brilliantly colored, almost glowing in the afternoon sunrays that danced on the ocean floor. "Aw, it's so pretty. And it looks tasty."

"Don't try it, man," said the anemone. "That's a mantis shrimp."

"What do you know?" said the octopus. "You can't even move."

"Not true," said the anemone. "I can slide. I'm just very slow. But I'm telling you, if you go after that mantis shrimp, you're going to regret it."

"Whatever," said the octopus, following the rainbow-colored stomatopod in what it thought was a sneaky manner.

The mantis shrimp dove into its hole. Rats, thought the octopus. Too slow. But the mantis shrimp quickly popped out again, facing the octopus. It spread its claws wide.

"Leave now," said the mantis shrimp. "If you do, I won't hurt you."

"Oh wow, the little shrimp is gonna hurt me," said the octopus. "I'm so afraid."

"I'm not a shrimp," said the mantis shrimp. "I'm just named after one."

"Wow, a little touchy about the name, Shrimpy?" said the octopus.

"You've forgotten the other part of my name. I'm also named after the mantis."

"Oh yeah?" said the octopus, edging forward. "Why's that?"

"Because of these."

The mantis shrimp darted forward and punched the octopus with a claw accelerating faster than a .22-caliber bullet. The four-inch creature hit with a force of 200 pounds.

"Wait, what?" said the octopus, dazed. "How can a shrimp hit that hard?"

"I'm not a shrimp. I'm a mantis shrimp." The stomatopod struck the octopus again.

Mantis shrimp live in warm, shallow waters in the Indian and Pacific Oceans between Hawaii and Africa. Most live to be three to six, but some can live up to twenty years. Though most are around four inches long, some species grow to be as much as eighteen inches.

Though they're rarely very large, the creatures are deadly predators, preying on crabs, fish, worms, and yes, shrimp. Mantis shrimp species are separated into two violent groups: spearers and smashers. Spearers have sharper claws with barbs on them that they use to (you guessed it) spear their prey. The smashers have blunter, club-like claws that they use to (yeah, you guessed it again) smash their prey to death.

For both groups, their claws are so fast that the super-speed creates cavitation bubbles between the claw and the target. When these bubbles collapse, they create a shock wave that can kill or stun the mantis shrimp's prey even if the stomatopod misses its shot. If they do hit, the prey gets smacked with the double-punch of both claw and shock wave. Mantis shrimp can take on prey far larger than themselves using these tactics. Even octopi.

Many species of mantis shrimp sport incredibly vibrant colors, with the peacock mantis shrimp looking like an underwater rainbow. Not only are mantis shrimp colorful, but they also have the most complex eyes in the animal kingdom.

Human beings have three types of photoreceptor cells in their eyes. Mantis shrimp have between twelve and sixteen. They're able to see tons of colors that we can't even imagine. Scientists are currently studying mantis shrimp eyes to develop our own visual technology.

These stomatopods aren't often kept in zoos or aquariums because they have a nasty tendency to kill the other creatures in the tank. They also require special aquariums because they can punch through normal tank glass.

Sometimes they ride into a tank by accident, though. Certain species of mantis shrimp are rock burrowers, and they'll get picked up with a rock intended to be a decoration for an aquarium full of friendly clown fish and hermit crabs.

The shrimp comes out of his rock burrow and goes to work feasting on all its tank mates. They're quite difficult to catch. They're good at hiding and, even if you find them, you have to be careful that they don't punch or chop off one of your fingers when you try to get them out.

"I-I'm gonna go now," said the octopus.

"I think that's a good idea," said the mantis shrimp.

The octopus moved away. The mantis shrimp sprang up and punched it one more time right between the eyes for good measure.

The octopus groaned. "You win. You win. Just let me go."

"Don't come back," said the mantis shrimp. "I'm not fond of visitors that aren't dinner."

A GOOPY CATASTROPHE

It was a warm day for January in Boston, business as usual. Horses clopped through the streets. A man took a nap after having worked late in the Pen and Pencil Club Saloon the night before. A group of firefighters played cards over their lunch in the firehouse. Children wandered the street.

"Well, there's good pickings today," said Tony as he picked up a few pieces of firewood.

"It was better last week," said his sister, Maria. "With that cart that got smashed up in that accident, we had all the wood we wanted."

"What are you looking at, Pasquale?" Tony asked. Their friend stared up at the fifty-food-high holding tank above them. It was groaning as if tired.

"What's in there?" Pasquale asked.

"Dad told me it's molasses," said Tony.

"Molasses?" said Maria. "Who needs that much molasses?"

Tony shrugged.

"Is it supposed to make those noises?" Pasquale asked.

"What noises?" said Maria.

"Those creaking and groaning sounds," said Pasquale.

"Oh, it always does that," said Tony. "Don't mind it. It's lasted this long. I suppose it'll last a while longer."

The ground shook, and a great roar filled the air. No one even had time to look and see what it was. A huge wave of molasses, at least fifteen feet high rushed through Boston's North End.

It swallowed up horses, knocked buildings from their foundations and laid them flat, buckled the steel support beams of the elevated train, and pulled people into its gooey depths.

The man who had been napping woke up in several feet of molasses. The card-playing firemen were trapped in an air pocket of a molasses-flooded room on the first floor of the firehouse. Rescue workers cut away at the floor above the men for several hours before managing to pull them free.

The molasses holding tank belonged to United States Industrial Alcohol (USIA). Back in 1919, molasses was fermented to produce alcohol. The tank was built in 1915 when alcohol was needed for the manufacture of weapons. After the war ended, the alcohol was used to make alcoholic beverages, which were in high demand at the time.

The tank had been shoddily built from the beginning. It routinely sprang leaks and creaked and groaned eerily. Though people complained, USIA didn't do anything about it. Then, on January 15, 1919, the tank decided it had had enough. It burst, spilling 2.3 million gallons of molasses. Molasses is much denser and heavier than water, which made a wave of molasses much more destructive than a wave of other liquid would have been. The wave destroyed several city blocks, wrecked businesses and homes, and injured 150 people. Several horses and twenty-one people died as well.

The cleanup was particularly nasty since molasses hardens in cold temperatures.

Residents of the ruined North End pitched in to clean up the mess. Three hundred people gathered to carry away debris and wreckage. Firefighters brought in brooms, saws, and saltwater pumps to scrub away the remaining molasses. Boston Harbor remained a murky brown until the following summer, when the color eventually faded away. However, North Enders talking about the disaster years later still said that on hot summer days they could still smell the sweet, sticky smell of warm molasses in the air.

THE GREAT EMU WAR

The farmer stared over his ruined wheat crops in despair. He'd repaired his fences just last week, but it was impossible to keep them out. They were too big, too strong. He didn't know what to do.

He sighed. He'd fought in World War I. The Australian government had given him a plot of land to farm afterward. Wheat farming sounded peaceful. It sounded like a nice rest after the spraying bullets, the trenches, the bloodshed. He'd thought he'd have a rest. And it had been restful at first.

But now, in the middle of the Great Depression and the falling of wheat prices, things had been hard. And now, he'd discovered an enemy that rivaled those he fought in the Great War: the emu. They'd been breaking through his fences and laying huge plots of wheat flat for weeks. Now, it looked like he wouldn't have a crop to harvest at the end of this season. What could he do then? How could he live? Something had to be done.

In 1932, a huge number of farmers came to the Australian government complaining of the emu (pronounced ee-moo) problem. The huge, flightless birds kept breaking through their fences and destroying their crops. The government had wanted to produce more wheat to stimulate the economy during the Depression, but this was looking impossible with the emu problem. The farmers wanted troops to come out and kill the birds.

Amazingly, the government responded, though not with great enthusiasm. They sent exactly three men: Major Gwynydd Purves Wynne-Aubrey Meredith (yes, he had that many names) to command the mission and Sergeant S. McMurray and Gunner J. O'Halloran to man the gun. They were equipped with two machine guns and 10,000 rounds of ammunition.

The following fight was an epic failure. First, the men tried to shoot the emus when they were out of range, which scared them all off. They only managed to kill perhaps a little more than a dozen birds that day, even though local villagers tried to herd them together and push them toward the shooters. The emus tended to split up and travel in small groups, which made them much more difficult to shoot.

A few days later, the soldiers tried to ambush about 1,000 emus at a dam. The gun jammed up after killing only twelve birds, and they were unable to shoot anymore.

They tried several more strategies, but Major Meredith started to believe that these birds were smarter than they looked. He talked of how they seemed to have watch-birds in each of their small groups who would warn the other birds that they were coming.

The soldiers tried to attach one of the guns to a truck so they could keep up with the birds, but the truck wasn't fast enough. The ground was too rough to be able to shoot anyway.

After about a month, Meredith, McMurray, and O'Halloran were ordered to go home and stop chasing the emus. Opinions vary about how many of the emus they actually killed. One report said only fifty. The settlers said it was 500. Both numbers were considered unsatisfactory.

The emu crop attacks continued, and the farmers kept complaining. With support from a popular political figure, Meredith, McMurray, and O'Halloran were sent out once again. They did better this time, killing an average of one hundred birds a week. They were called home again after another month, this time claiming that they'd killed around 3,500 birds.

As word spread about the emu war, many conservationists became angry. Some called the birds "rare," and said they must be protected. Others called it the "mass destruction of the birds." The government decided to change their strategy. Instead of sending military men, they put a bounty on each emu's head. In 1934, 57,034 emus were killed for the bounty in just six months.

The farmer raised his shotgun and fired it three times. One bird flopped to the ground while its companions took off running. He sighed, thinking about dragging the enormous bird to town hall to collect the bounty. Emus were less trouble now than they used to be, but they were still trouble enough, he thought.

DYING TO DISCOVER

Wearing lead suits and face masks, they slowly gathered the woman's belongings. Papers, furniture, cookbooks, and clothing, they carted them all away. One couldn't touch them. They couldn't be stored in an attic or storage room without doing damage. What possessions they wouldn't destroy, they would seal into lead-lined boxes, not to be opened without serious warning to those who wanted to see. These materials were highly radioactive. Handle at your own risk.

This is what happened to Marie Curie's possessions after her death in 1934. Curie was the first woman to win a Nobel Prize and the first person to win two of them. What did she do that was so important? She studied and discovered radioactive elements and their effects.

Curie was born in Poland but went to college in Paris, where she studied physics and mathematics. She met a professor, Pierre Curie, while studying there. The two scientists married a year later. She also studied under Henri Becquerel, who had recently discovered a new phenomenon.

Becquerel was trying to learn about phosphorescence. He wrapped a photographic plate in black paper to block out visible light. He placed different elements on the plate, then exposed them to sunlight to see if they'd make an image on the plate. This worked for none of the elements except uranium. It left black marks on the plate.

He ran the experiment again, but the day was cloudy, and he didn't expect it to work. However, he was surprised to find uranium still blackened the plate. Becquerel had stumbled upon radiation, although he didn't call it that. He published his findings in a few journals and then went off to study something else.

Marie read his findings when she was looking for a topic to study for her doctoral thesis. She decided to see if she could find other elements that emitted the same invisible rays put out by uranium. Her new husband decided to join her in the quest. Together, they discovered both radium and polonium, and Marie came up with the name "radioactivity."

Radiation has a number of uses. Doctors use it to perform x-rays, CAT scans, and CT scans. Radiation therapy is frequently used to treat cancer. Scientists track radioactive substances in order to study paths of air and water pollution.

Archaeologists use radioactive substances to estimate the ages of fossils and other ancient objects. Radiation is used in the industrial world to kill germs and remove toxic pollutants. Agricultural workers expose plant seeds to certain types of radiation in order to strengthen the plants. And that's not to mention the microwave, the nuclear power plant, and, of course, the atomic bomb. The discovery of radiation has changed, and will continue to change, our world dramatically.

After winning her second Nobel prize, Marie Curie was able to convince the French government to back her Radium Institute, which would conduct studies on radiation's uses in medicine, chemistry, and physics. This institute ended up producing several other Nobel winners including Marie's own daughter, Irène.

Though Curie was, by nature, one who wanted to continue studying and discovering, she took a break from her research with the onset of World War I. X-ray machines had been invented a few years before, but Curie saw the need for them to be portable so they could be used on the front lines.

So, she invented the radiological car and set to work raising funds to have enough of them to supply the Allies' needs. Curie learned to drive, look after the vehicles, learned human anatomy, and set out with her daughter Irène to help wounded soldiers on the battlefront. By the end, she had trained up nearly 150 women to operate these front-line X-ray vehicles.

After the war, Marie traveled and raised funding and support for her research. In addition to her Nobels, she was given a position on the International Committee on Intellectual Cooperation, The International Atomic Weights Committee, and she received the Cameron Prize for Therapeutics from the University of Edinburgh.

Though she accomplished much, she didn't live to be very old. Curie had refused to acknowledge the danger of the elements she studied. When she did pass away her body was found to be so radioactive that her coffin was lined with an inch of lead to contain the radioactivity.

Her notebooks are still radioactive to this day and will need to stay contained for many more years.

FROM FIELD TO WASHTUB TO KITCHEN TO MILLIONAIRE

As Sarah pulled the comb through her hair, a large clump stayed in it. Looking down, she sighed.

"Here, Mama," said A'Lelia, taking the comb from her hand, "you pull it too hard. Let me do it." Her daughter gently brushed what was left of her mother's hair.

"Doesn't make a difference," said Sarah. "It's all going to fall out soon unless I find some treatment for it."

"Have you asked Uncle James or Uncle Alex?"

Sarah laughed. "Child, your uncles know how to cut a person's hair off, not how to make it stay on."

"Well still," A'Lelia said, "maybe you should ask them."

Sarah did and began her journey to become a millionaire.

Sarah Breedlove was born in 1867 in Louisiana. Her parents, brothers, and sisters had been slaves, but the Emancipation Proclamation had freed them. Sarah was the first one in the family to be born free.

Freedom didn't mean her life was easy, though. Both Sarah's parents died by the time she was seven, and she went to live with her sister in Mississippi. She married at fourteen years old and soon had her daughter, Lelia, later to be called A'Lelia. Her husband died two years later.

Sarah moved to St. Louis where three of her brothers were barbers. She got a job washing clothes. While living there, she was active in the church and got to know African American women who were well educated and active members of their community. She began to wonder if there was more for her in life than being a washwoman. Around this time, she developed a nasty scalp condition that gave her heavy dandruff and caused her hair to fall out.

Sarah asked her brothers about it, and they taught her all they knew. Later she got a job as a saleswoman for the Poro Company, a business that sold hygiene and hair care products, particularly for African American women. Sarah learned more and more, eventually gaining the confidence to experiment with creating her own hair products.

She married a man named C. J. Walker and took up the name Madam C. J. Walker as her brand label. She started out selling her products door-to-door. Her husband was a newspaper man and knew about advertising. He used his marketing skills to help her put ads in the newspapers. She began to hire agents to sell for her. She traveled to promote her product, leaving A'Lelia to take care of her in-town business while she was away.

The business continued to grow. Sarah built a factory and established many haircare training schools, employing thousands of women.

Her fortune grew, and she built a mansion in Harlem. She became a philanthropist, spreading her money far and wide. She gave funds to build a YMCA in Indianapolis. She funded different educational institutions, trying to make it possible for young African American people to be educated. She also donated to and supported the arts in her community.

Sarah was also a feminist and political activist. She loved to tell her story, how she had come from a family of slaves, had been orphaned, and had worked hard to make herself a successful businesswoman. She wanted to inspire others to dream big as well.

She was friends with important activists of the day, including Booker T. Washington and W. E. B. Du Bois. She held a place on the executive committee of the National Association for the Advancement of Colored People (NAACP) in New York and donated what would now be in the ball park of $150,000 to their anti-lynching fund. This was the biggest gift from one person the NAACP had ever received.

Her company is still thriving, and you can buy products from MADAM, by Madam C. J. Walker online. Her factory in Indianapolis has been turned into Walker Theater and several books and even a TV show have been made about the life of the first self-made female millionaire in the United States. But none of it would have ever happened if she hadn't started to go bald.

The men rode the truck inside the mountain for another day's work. They were miners. Some of them were old-timers, having mined Chile's copper veins for decades. Some were young and inexperienced. For all, it seemed an average day. That is, until the ground began to vibrate, and then to shake. An enormous explosion sounded. Dust and grit flew up into the air, filling the tunnels and blinding the miners.

When the dust finally settled, the men gathered, shining their headlamps around to try to understand what had happened. They saw a rock, a megablock, 770,000 tons, as tall as a forty-five-story building, covering the mine's entrance. They were trapped.

The miners tried to escape using ventilation shafts, but the safety ladders were missing. They formed an underground democracy: one man, one vote, and planned what they would do. Gathering emergency food rations that were made to last only three days, the men rationed themselves just two spoonfuls of tuna, a sip of milk, and one to two cookies every day or so.

On the surface, the rescue was underway. Not knowing the miners' whereabouts in the mine or if they were even alive, rescuers started trying to access the tunnels and shafts the miners normally used. All of these were blocked. They tried to break through using heavy machinery, but they had to quit when it seemed like it might cause more of the mine to collapse.

The miners' family members arrived at the site and waited to see what would happen. After several days, they started bringing in tents and other camping gear. The rescuers joined them in their camp once they realized they wouldn't be getting the miners out anytime soon. A tent city formed.

Relatives of the victims barraged the rescuers and law enforcement with questions about their loved ones. Catholicism is the main religion in Chile, so many of the families prayed and lit candles for the lost miners. They called their camp "Campo Esperanza": "Camp Hope."

Rescuers drilled holes in the rock, seeing if they could communicate with the miners somehow. After seventeen days of drilling, one of the drills came back with a message taped to its end: "All thirty-three of us are fine in the shelter." The men were two-fifths of a mile underground and three miles into the mineshaft.

The rescuers used their searching drill holes to send food and supplies down to the miners. They sent down a camera so the trapped men could send messages to the world outside. In the forty-minute video the miners created, they seemed upbeat and positive. They looked mostly healthy, though thin.

The rescuers created a plan to get the men out based on other successful mineshaft rescues. The idea was to drill a hole to the men and create a man-sized capsule to pull them out one by one. It was slow work. They had to build and drill carefully to prevent further collapses.

The miners continued to live in their isolation. One of them was a pastor as well as a miner, and they regularly prayed and held religious services. They worked out. They sent video journals to those above ground. They tried to stay optimistic and avoid getting on each other's nerves.

On October 13, sixty-nine days after the mine's collapse, longer than any other humans had survived being trapped underground, the capsule went into the mine. A rescuer rode down inside to help the miners make their exit. When the miners saw him, they hugged him and celebrated.

One by one, the miners climbed into the capsule. The journey took about ten to twenty minutes stuffed inside the tiny compartment. When they reached the surface, they were greeted by cheers and crying family members and the president of Chile himself.

All thirty-three men made it safely out of the mine. They were mostly in good health, some in better shape than when they'd gone down because of the extra time they'd had to exercise. The mine did take its toll on them, though. All but one of them suffered from Post-Traumatic Stress Disorder, forcing many of them out of the mining industry. Though their lives were difficult upon leaving the mine, they did have their lives, more than most could expect after being trapped underground for sixty-nine days.

JOSEPH MERRICK, A SHORT AND CURIOUS LIFE

You're on Whitechapel Road in London. It is 1884. A man stands on the side of the street calling. A crowd surrounds him.

"Come one and all!" he says. "Only a few coins, and I'll show you someone stupendous!"

You think, *why not? I don't have anything else to do right now.*

The man ushers you inside. Posters of a creature crossed between a man and an elephant line the walls. A bed stands in the center of the room with a curtain drawn around it. The man from outside steps to the side of the bed.

"Ladies and gentlemen," he says, "I would like to introduce Mr. Joseph Merrick, the Elephant Man. Before doing so I ask you please to prepare yourselves—Brace yourselves up to witness one who is probably the most remarkable human being ever to draw the breath of life."

He pulls back the curtain, and you see a man. At least, you're pretty sure it's a man. He sits on the bed. Yes, that's a head on his shoulders, but it's huge, about three times the size of a normal head. Growths cover his forehead and the right side of his face, nearly covering his mouth and right eye. His right hand and arm are also enormous, his fingers thick and doughy. His left arm looks completely normal. Growths coat his chest and back. His eyes are on the ground. He doesn't look at you.

"The Elephant Man," says the showman, "like all of us, has a story. Pamphlets of his autobiography are available for only the smallest of fees."

You buy a pamphlet, and on your walk home, you read of Joseph Merrick's life.

Merrick was born in Leicester, England in 1884. The tumors didn't start to appear until he was about five years old. His family attributed his deformity to his mother being frightened by an elephant while pregnant with him.

Merrick went to school like other children, stopping at thirteen to begin work. He rolled cigars at a factory for two years before his deformity progressed, making his right arm barely useable. He became a licensed salesman, but people were too frightened at the sight of him to open their doors. Even if they did, Merrick's deformity impaired his speech, making it difficult to understand him. His father kicked him out when he was unable to support himself.

At seventeen, Merrick spent four years in a workhouse. He then thought perhaps he could get work in a human novelty show. He contacted comedian Sam Torr, who came to have a look at him. Torr thought Merrick might be a success and arranged for a few managers to take Merrick around the country as a traveling show.

Merrick traveled in the warmer months and settled in an empty shop on Whitechapel Road in London for the winter. While he was there, a man named Frederick Treves came to see him.

Treves took Merrick to the hospital to examine him, measuring him and taking pictures, hoping to learn about his illness. Merrick eventually asked to stop going, saying that at the hospital he "felt like an animal in a cattle market."

Merrick's managers took him on a tour around Europe when human curiosity shows became less acceptable in England. On this tour, Merrick's manager stole all his savings and abandoned him in Brussels.

Merrick managed to get back to London, but his prospects were dismal. He couldn't work. The only workhouse where he could stay was in Leicester, nearly one hundred miles away. A policeman came to his aid. Finding Frederick Treves's card in Merrick's clothes, the policeman called him. Treves had Merrick driven to London Hospital in a cab.

It was quickly realized that Merrick needed long-term care, but London Hospital said it didn't have room for incurable cases.

Treves wrote to the local paper asking for advice on how to care for Merrick, and received an enthusiastic response. London citizens and celebrities provided the necessary finances for the hospital to set up permanent quarters for Merrick.

Treves visited Merrick daily and stayed with him for a few hours on Sundays, eventually coming to understand his speech. The rest of Merrick's life was relatively peaceful. He wrote poetry, went on a few trips to the country, and built model structures out of cardstock.

He died at twenty-seven. His skeleton was preserved for scientific study and can be viewed privately at London's Queen Mary University.

A MYSTICAL SCIENTIST

Perhaps you know George Washington Carver as the guy who invented peanut butter and a whole bunch of other plant products. Sounds like a pretty practical guy, doesn't he? But did you know that he was also a bit of a mystic?

Carver talked constantly throughout his life about how his inventions were the result of God showing him what to do. According to Carver, God talked to him quite regularly, starting when he was very young.

At one point in his childhood, Carver developed a strong desire for a pocketknife. He was a highly inventive child and no doubt had all kinds of ideas about what he could do with it. However, Mr. and Mrs. Carver, the frugal couple who raised him, didn't like to spend money. He knew they would have no interest in getting him a knife.

One night, he had a dream. He saw, in that dream, a half-eaten watermelon, and sticking out of the watermelon was a knife. The next day, Carver was wandering outside. He found the watermelon, and there was the pocketknife sticking out of it. Is that weird or what? Later in life, Carver came to believe that God had revealed the knife to him through this dream.

As an adult, Carver came up with a version of crop rotation to help reinvigorate the soil in the South. The soil was depleted as a result of years and years of cotton crops. Cotton strips soil of its nutrients, and this results in lousy crops of cotton and nearly everything else. Peanuts are one plant that gives nutrients back to the soil. Carver started telling farmers that they should do a crop rotation, planting peanuts every other year. Carver told the farmers that they could eat the peanuts or feed them to their animals.

Farmers took his advice, and the result was an overabundance of peanuts. The farmers had way more than they knew what to do with. So, carver set about finding uses for the peanuts. He discovered more than 300!

He was asked to speak to a Committee in Washington, D.C. He had been scheduled to speak for ten minutes, but ended up talking for an hour and forty-five minutes about all the things that could be done with a peanut plant.

The committee was astonished. The chairman asked Carver how he'd learned all this about the peanut. Carver told him, "From an old book."

"What book?" asked the chairman.

"The Bible," Carver said.

"Does the Bible tell about peanuts?" asked the chairman.

"No sir," Carver said, "but it tells about the God who made the peanut. I asked Him to show me what to do with the peanut, and He did."

God told Carver that He'd given mankind peanuts and all plants for their use. Then God sent Carver to the laboratory, to experiment and unleashed all the properties of peanuts. Most scientists would say that Carver used his mind to discover these facts, but Carver saw it all as God speaking to him and telling him what to do.

Carver also talked of how he would go out to nature and receive these revelations from God through nature: "All my life," he said, "I have risen regularly at four o'clock and have gone into the woods and talked with God. There He gives me my orders for the day. Alone there with the things I love most, I gather specimens and study the great lessons nature is so eager to teach us all."

Carver attributed nearly everything he'd learned to revelations from God. He thought of nature as a form of God's revelation, and he believed that God spoke to him through it. Out of his hundreds of inventions, he patented only three. He didn't think he could sell his ideas to people when God have given them to him for free.

THE CURSE OF THE SQUIRREL-CAT-MONKEY-THING

As the sun set, Rindra poked the fire. "Better look out," she said, staring at her two younger siblings with solemn eyes. "The sun's going down."

"So what?" said Ravaka.

"The aye-ayes only come out at night," Rindra said.

"I repeat," said Ravaka, "so what?"

"You don't know about the aye-ayes?" Rindra said, peering at them over the flames.

"I saw one hanging from a tree on the edge of the market last week," said Andro proudly. "It was dead. Dad says they keep away evil spirits."

Rindra laughed a mirthless laugh. "They only keep spirits away when they're dead."

Andro shivered and hugged his knees.

"Didn't you know?" Rindra said. "Aye-ayes carry evil spirits inside of them. They say that, if you see an aye-aye, it means someone in your village will die. The only way to keep it from happening is to kill it. If it's not killed, the aye-aye will sneak into your room at night, stretch out its skinny middle finger," Rindra stretched out her finger, "and pierce your heart while you sleep." She stabbed her finger into Ravaka's arm.

"Ow!" her sister said.

Andro's eyes were wide. "Really?" he asked.

"No, not really," Ravaka said, rubbing her arm and glaring at Rinda. "She's just trying to scare you. Don't believe anything she says."

"Maybe she's right, Andro," said Rindra, standing, "but maybe she's not. Either way, the aye-ayes come out at night." She stared into the forest line that stood so close to their house. "Just look out," she said, turning to go inside.

Andro gulped and stared into the trees.

The aye-aye is one of the weirdest mammals around. Scientists have struggled to categorize it since they first found it in Madagascar in the 1700s. Originally, they thought it was related to the squirrel because of its long, constantly growing teeth and the appearance of its fur, tail, and toes. But its face and head shape are similar to those of felines. Now they say it's a lemur and categorize it with monkeys, but scientists have no idea what its closest primate relative is. It's just too different to fit well in any of the categories.

Aye-ayes aren't just strange in their appearance. To get their food, they mix bat and woodpecker hunting tactics. They have an especially thin claw (which they also use to pick their noses and eat their snot) that they use to tap rapidly on trees. The sound of the taps allows them to use echolocation, a process used to find objects by listening to the sound waves bouncing off them, to find their dinner.

When they've located their prey within the tree, they use their rodent teeth to gnaw a hole in the tree. They then reach inside with their especially long claw to grab their prey. They have six digits instead of five, having developed what scientists call a pseudo-thumb to help them grip.

Aye-ayes are largely solitary creatures. They do interact with each other occasionally when they happen to run into each other. But for the most part, they swing alone through their branchy kingdom in the dark, spending about eighty percent of their waking hours on the hunt.

Like many of the most interesting animals in our world, aye-ayes are endangered. Their forest homes are being chopped down for logging purposes and to make way for sugar cane and coconut plantations. Farmers kill them, claiming that they're protecting their crops, though there's no real evidence that aye-ayes hurt crops.

They're also killed for superstitious reasons. Some residents of Madagascar consider them bad omens, frequently killing them and hanging them up to ward off the evil luck they bring. Some in the Sakalava people group spread the story that aye-ayes will sneak into houses and murder sleepers by using their long, thin fingers to pierce their hearts.

Leaves rustled in the woods, and Andro jumped.

"You big baby," Ravaka said. "I told you; she was just teasing. The aye-ayes aren't going to bother you."

She sat with her back to the woods. A hand clapped onto her shoulder, and then something sharp jabbed into her chest. Ravaka screamed, falling off the stump of wood she'd been sitting on.

She turned to see Rindra, rolling on the ground with laughter. Andro also covered his mouth with his hand, giggling.

"Y-you say you're not scared," Rindra panted between laughs, "but you jump higher than a toad riding a firework at the slightest touch!"

Ravaka stood and icily walked into the house, her sister's laugh echoing behind her in the dark.

28TH TRY'S A CHARM

Ted walked down the street with his manuscript tucked under his arm, head down, discouragement coating him like a fog. Twenty-seven. His children's book had now been rejected twenty-seven times. He liked the book. He thought it was very good. Shoot, it was way better than a lot of the books he saw in the kids' bookstores these days. But no one else seemed to think so.

Ted sighed. He must be wrong. Maybe he didn't know what a good kids' book was. He'd go back to advertising. Or maybe he'd go work at a dry cleaner. He'd heard there was good money in that.

Yes, he'd give up. He'd walk straight home and throw this book into his apartment's incinerator, let it turn to ash along with his hopes of becoming a children's author. Give it up and start something new. He was only thirty-three. He had his whole life ahead of him. He'd go find something else to do.

"Well hi, Ted!"

Ted looked up to see his friend standing in front him, smiling like he'd just had the greatest day of his life. He stopped walking. "Oh, hi Mike. How are you?"

"Just great, Ted. You know what I'm doing? I'm walking home from my first day of work at Vanguard Press."

"Vanguard Press?" Ted said. "The publisher?"

"Yeah, isn't it great! I'm an editor in the children's section."

Ted couldn't help but laugh. "Are you now?"

"Why yes, I am. And I'd like to know what's funny about it?" Mike looked a bit offended.

"Oh, nothing," said Ted shaking his head. He held up his manuscript. "I just got my manuscript back from a different publishing company. They rejected me."

"You wrote a book, Ted?" Mike looked very interested.

"Yeah, but not a good one," Ted sighed. "Don't tell anyone, but this is my twenty-seventh rejection. I'm headed home to throw it into the fire. Maybe I'll go back into advertising."

Mike didn't smile. "Let me see, won't you Ted?"

Ted sighed again. "I guess twenty-eight rejections is about the same as twenty-seven. Here."

Mike flipped through the pages.

"I was going to call it A Story That No One Can Beat," Ted said.

Mike nodded, kept reading, smiling his way through the story, sometimes laughing out loud. Then he looked up at Ted. "You know, this is a story that no one can beat. Not a great title, though. I'd try to find something a little more quippy. But the story is great!"

Ted stared at him, unable to speak.

Mike laughed again. "Come on, Ted. You're not saying twenty-seven publishers passed you up on this."

"That's exactly what I'm saying."

"But the kids would love the pictures alone! And your rhyme and rhythm are catchy. And the parents will love that it tells their kids not to exaggerate. It's great, Ted. It's really great. You can't throw this one in the fire. Come with me back to the office right now, and we're going to sign you a contract for this book."

"You're not serious, Mike."

"I'm as serious as this book is ridiculous," said Mike.

They went back to Mike's office, and Ted signed a contract selling his book that very day. They renamed the book "And to Think That I Saw It on Mulberry Street".

Ted didn't write under his own name. He used a name he'd invented in college after he got kicked out of his position as editor of the school newspaper. Ted continued to write for the paper under a false name. He took his mother's maiden name, Suess, and made himself, fictitiously, what his father had always wanted him to be: a doctor. Thus, the name Dr. Suess was born.

Ted went on to write and illustrate more than sixty books. He became a loved children's book writer and his books sold over 600 million copies and were translated into more than twenty languages before he died.

He commented later in life on how incredibly lucky that chance meeting with Mike was. He said, "If I had been going down the other side of Madison Avenue, I'd be in the dry-cleaning business today." It just goes to show, if at first you don't succeed, you should try at least twenty-seven more times.

OFF TO THE FEATHER RACES

"I can't see!" said Shanyah, straining on her tiptoes to see over the man standing in front of her.

"Me neither," said Kametrick. "We've gotta stand on the bench."

They climbed up and peered over the adults' shoulders. The racetrack spread before them, long lanes of opportunity stretching around and around and around. And there were the jockeys, wrestling with their animals behind the gate.

The crowd cheered as the man raised his pistol and yelled into his megaphone.

"Riders, mount your ostriches!"

The riders fought to mount the huge birds, many of which did not want to have people on their backs. Eventually every jockey rested precariously on top of his ostrich.

"On your mark," said the man with the megaphone, "get set, go!" He shot the pistol, and the riders took off. Or tried to. Many ostriches still did not want to race. One spun around and around, trying to lose its rider through sheer dizziness. Another kept going back and forth in short bursts, seeing if this would set it free from the huge weight on its back. Jockeys began to lose their mounts.

Several ostriches did take off down the racetrack, sprinting as fast as horses. Along the way, several more riders lost their grip and fell to the ground. The crowd roared with laughter.

"Do you think the jockeys win because they're good?" Shanyah said, "or just because their ostriches like them better?"

Kametrick cackled as another jockey bit the dust. "Seems like nice is a lot more important than fast!"

Ostrich racing has been around for more than a hundred years. It got its start, as one might guess, in Africa.

We don't quite know when Africans started racing ostriches, but the sport really caught fire when ostrich farms started showing up in the United States, particularly in Florida.

Ostriches were valuable because their feathers were highly fashionable at the time.

By 1890, ostrich racing was common in Jacksonville, St. Petersburg, and St. Augustine. Both locals and tourists had the chance to race the birds.

Though these races were popular in the early 1900s, they're less common now. With the rise of animal rights activists, people became concerned for the birds. In the wild, they never carry anything as heavy as humans, and there are concerns that doing it regularly might lead to injury or weakening of joints and bones.

However, ostrich racing hasn't died out entirely. There's a big Ostrich Festival in Chandler, Arizona, every year that hosts an ostrich race. You can race an ostrich in South Africa if you go to Oudtshoorn. There are hundreds of thousands of ostriches there, and, when they're not being used commercially for their meat, eggs, and hides, they are used to entertain tourists.

Nowadays, ostrich riders are not allowed to be heavier than 165 pounds. But racing an ostrich may not always be all it's cracked up to be. You have to understand from the beginning that the races are far from competitive, and you're quite likely to take a tumble off the enormous fowls.

Ostriches also shouldn't be treated as though they're totally tame. Though they can be handled safely, when they're scared or provoked, the seven-to-nine-foot, 140-320-pound birds can be dangerous. Aside from being the fastest land birds, they can pack kicks strong enough to kill lions, and their claws are sharp, too (just ask Johnny Cash). Though the ones on farms will typically be tamer, ostriches, like all animals, deserve to be treated respectfully.

There were only two riders left on their way to the finish line, holding tight, the wind whooshing past them. Then, without warning, one of the ostriches turned around and started running the other way. The winner raised his hands in the air in triumph as he passed the finished line, promptly falling off the ostrich onto his rump.

Shanyah and Kametrick were dying laughing.

"Did you-did you see his face?" Shenyah cackled, falling behind the bench and not ceasing to laugh. "It was like those cartoon characters who get anvils dropped on their heads!"

"I-I don't think I ever want to race an ostrich," Kametrick gasped, "but I sure do love watching other people do it."

MY PIRATES CAN BE PIRATES AS LONG AS THEY WANT TO!

"How do you think this will go?" asked Pompeius, as he and his companion mounted the steps to the queen's home.

"I don't know," said Spurius. "Even if she agrees to tell them to stop the plundering, they'll probably just ignore her. Would you listen if you were ruled by a queen?"

Pompeius laughed. "I would sooner betray Rome than be ruled by a queen."

They stopped talking as they approached the guards standing at the entrance. Telling them their business, they were ushered into the throne room.

There the queen sat, advisors surrounding her, heatedly discussing something or other. The guards led the diplomats up to her, one of the guards standing directly in front of her. She held up her hand to silence the men around her.

"Yes, Barteo? What is it?"

"These men would like a word with you, Queen Teuta. They have come from Rome."

She raised her eyebrows. "Thank you, Barteo." She turned to the men. "What word would you like to have with me?"

Pompeius handed a scroll to Teuta, saying, "The Roman Senate has sent us to discuss with you the villainous, barbaric, and murderous plundering of your Illyrian pirates on all trading vessels that sail along this section of the Adriatic Sea. The Senate wishes to tell you that you must reign in your pirates, and they also wish to tell you they expect repayment for all its losses at the hands of your pirates."

Teuta scanned the scroll, and then looked up at the men. She looked irritated, as if she shouldn't be bothered with matters so trivial. "You must understand that piracy is not illegal in Illyria. If your ships cannot defend themselves against our pirates, you must suffer the consequences."

Spurius flared up. "How dare you? We are sent by the Roman Republic. We can squash your little Illyrian realm with our little finger. Come to your senses, woman, or be prepared to reap the consequences. You do not," his voice lowered, "want to be at war with Rome."

Teuta stood. "And perhaps you, man, do not want to be at war with me. Perhaps you need to come to your senses before insulting the ruler of the mighty realm of Illyria." The guards and the advisors cheered. "Barteo!"

"Yes, Queen?"

"Execute this man!"

"What?" cried Spurius, in terror.

"And what of his comrade, Queen?"

She glanced at Pompeius as if he were barely worth her time. She shrugged. "Throw him in the dungeon."

"Yes, Queen Teuta."

"You'll live to regret this, Teuta!" Spurius called, as they dragged him away.

"Not nearly as much as you will," she said, sitting back down with a grim smile on her lips.

Queen Teuta ruled in Illyria, a region along the coast of the Adriatic Sea north of Greece, from 231-228/227 BC.

She was a regent, really. Her stepson was only two when his father died, so Teuta took over the region until he was of age.

Her husband, before his death, had been working to expand the country, taking over part of Greece's coast in his last great battle.

Teuta continued his conquests for expansion and managed to conquer the cities of Dyrrachium and Phoenice in Greece.

Illyria posed the biggest threat to others in its practice of unrestrained and deadly piracy. Piracy was not illegal in Illyria. Indeed, it was even encouraged because rulers received a portion of the pirates' booty. These pirates were an enormous bother to all trade ships passing along that section of the Adriatic.

Rome didn't enjoy having its trade ships looted, and it sent a couple of diplomats to tell Teuta to control her pirates and pay Rome back the damage the pirates had done. The meeting didn't go too well. Rome responded by sending huge fleets of ships and starting the first Illyrian War. Illyria was conquered, in the end, but not without a valiant struggle. Teuta was forced to surrender and pay Rome tribute.

It's hard to know how much of the historical account of Teuta's reign and life is to be believed. It was written by the Romans, who obviously didn't like her very much. She is portrayed very negatively in the accounts, but most people don't write nice things about their enemies.

THE MAN IN BLACK VS. THE ANGRY BIRD

Johnny finished his lunch, put his fork down, and pushed back his chair. "That was a mighty fine meal, Marjory."

"I'm glad you enjoyed it, sir. You're finished, then?" asked his maid, reaching for his plate.

"Yes, I believe I am."

"Is there anything else you need, sir?"

"No, no, I don't think so. I just want to go take a walk through the park."

"Yes, sir."

"Thank you, Marjory." He stood, shrugged on his coat, and strode through the door.

He was fond of his home in Bon Aqua in Tennessee. He only had it because that lying, cheating accountant had been stealing his money and buying properties with it. Pete had been caught in the end, and Johnny had sold all the properties to get his money back. All but this one. He loved Bon Aqua. He'd made it his home.

Johnny also loved animals, especially exotic ones. He'd decided to make a home for them here, too, and he had many kinds in his animal park. People thought he was foolish. What did a country music singer know about exotic animals? And Johnny had to admit that perhaps they'd been right to an extent. This winter had been brutal, and many of the animals from warmer climates were not doing well. Particularly the ostriches.

Johnny thought of yesterday when he'd had to carry a dead hen ostrich away from her mate. He'd tried to bring her inside to avoid the night air which would drop below zero degrees, but the hen had violently resisted. And she'd paid for it with her life. He'd never forget the look on her mate's face as Johnny dragged her away.

Last night hadn't been quite so cold though, and the other ostriches had gone into the barn as they should. Johnny didn't expect to find any casualties today.

Ah, there was the ostrich whose hen he'd dragged away the day before. He was all right. Just pecking away at the food the keeper had laid out for him. Then the ostrich saw him. It jumped onto the path in front of him, crouching, spreading his wings, hissing, ready to attack.

"Easy, fella," Johnny said, breaking into a sweat despite the cold, winter air. He backed up with his hands out. "I know you're sad about your lady, but it's not going to do you any good to hurt me."

The two stared at each other for a long time. Then the ostrich laid back his wings and wandered back off the path. Johnny walked on, but he was unnerved. His animals had never treated him this way. During his walk, Johnny saw a large stick lying on the ground. He knew that he'd have to pass back by that ostrich again on his way out. He picked up the stick and tossed it up and down a few times. He'd show that ostrich who was boss. He swung the stick. He wasn't going to be cowed by some bird, even if it was the biggest bird on earth.

Johnny finished his rounds through the park and came back to the path where he'd met the ostrich before. Sure enough, there he was. Once again, he splayed his wings, crouched, and hissed at Johnny. Johnny held up his stick, ready for whatever the bird could bring. Or so he thought.

Johnny swung the stick at the ostrich as hard as he could. But he hit only air. Then the bird pounced. Johnny knew ostriches couldn't fly, but, at this moment, this one could. It arced through the air at Johnny, its enormous talon aiming for Johnny's belly. It made contact, knocking him backward to land on a rock. Johnny heard a sickening cracking sound. The bird's talon scratched down his belly, running into his belt buckle.

Johnny groaned in pain, but he knew he couldn't give up the fight. This ostrich would slice him to ribbons in a minute if he didn't act quickly. He swung his stick wildly, back and forth, ignoring the pain as best he could. He heard a crack, and the bird screeched. He'd connected with its leg. The ostrich ran off, and Johnny began to yell for help.

One of the keepers came running. "What is it, Mr. Cash?"

"Dang ostrich got me!" he cried, covering his stomach with his hand. "Call an ambulance!"

Johnny Cash found that the ostrich had managed to do him significant damage, breaking two of his lower ribs with its talon strike, breaking another three ribs by knocking him onto a rock and scratching his stomach open down to his belt buckle. Cash attributed his survival to his quality clothing choice.

"If the belt hadn't been good and strong, with a solid belt buckle, he'd have killed me exactly the way he meant to."

THE LONG, LAZY LIFE

"What's up with you today, Rob?" asked the fish, floating listlessly near the bottom of the sea.

"Oh, you know, Bob," said his brother, floating nearby, "just hanging out."

"Do you think we should try doing something today?" Dob, their sister asked.

"Like what?" asked Bob.

"Oh, I don't know," said Dob. "We could...you know, float here. And wait for food to drift close to us so we can suck it into our mouths."

"I like that idea," said Rob. "Maybe we should move a little farther apart, so we can cover more area."

"That's a good thought," said Bob. "But, you know, then we'd have to move."

"Let's just see if the ocean pushes us further apart," said Dob.

"Great," said Bob. "Let's do that."

They floated.

The blobfish first rose to fame when it was nominated as a contestant in the world's ugliest species contest, a poll run by the Ugly Animal Preservation Society. Out of eleven nominations of animals like the proboscis monkey, with its enormous nose and bloated belly, and the Titicaca water frog, with its shrivelled-looking skin and its name meaning "aquatic scrotum frog", the blobfish won in a landslide, receiving more than 25% of the votes. People couldn't get over how ugly it was.

With a huge, bulbous nose, tiny, far-apart, black eyes, a parasite hanging onto the right side of its mouth, and its wide mouth turning far downward, the fish looked like an extremely sad cartoon character.

He (although no one is really sure if Mr. Blobby is a he) also seemed to have almost no skeleton and flesh made mostly of gelatinous material. No wonder they nicknamed the *Psychrolutes microporos* species "Blobfish."

A couple dozen scientists took a ship along the coasts of Australia and New Zealand, dragging nets deep, deep into the ocean.

They found the blobfish, which they soon named "Mr. Blobby," near the bottom of the net.

Oddly enough, the blobfish only looks as strange as he does because he was never meant to be in the open air. Fish of this kind live at depths between 330 and 9,200 feet. If you were to survive down there, you'd need a heavy-duty submarine to keep your bones and organs from being crushed. Blobfish don't have to worry about this; if you have hardly any skeleton and are basically made of Jell-O, you don't have to worry about getting squished. In fact, when a blobfish is in its deep-sea environment, it looks a lot more like a normal fish. Its body is made to be supported by water pressure instead of by a skeleton.

Most fish that don't live in the depths of the sea have swim bladders, which help them stay buoyant and move around without having to constantly hold themselves afloat like we do when we swim. If a blobfish had this, the bladder would (you guessed it) be crushed. Blobfish float along because their flesh has a slightly lower density than water. They bob above the bottom because the denser water pushes them up.

Blobfish have hardly any muscle, so they don't move much. In fact, it's believed that they don't really go out looking for food: they just wait for food to drift close to their mouths and then suck it in. They really are the couch potatoes of the ocean floor.

Life flows a little more slowly down there. Because of the lack of predators, some creatures at this depth can live to be more than 100 years old. This could be true of the blobfish. Why the hurry? They've got years and years ahead of them and nothing to do but drift and eat.

"I think we're actually drifting closer together," said Dob.

"Huh," said Rob.

"Slurp," said Bob. "Ugh. That mollusk was a little past its riper days."

"Maybe I'll take a nap," said Dob.

"We don't sleep," said Rob.

"Right," said Dob.

They floated.

THE ONE WHO NEVER GAVE UP

Saito exited the train and stretched. It had been a long day at the university. He was so tired of sitting. They'd told him when he had to leave the army for health reasons that he needed to get more exercise. He'd wanted to get a dog to go walking with him, but it was hard to find a good dog in Japan these days. Western breeds had made their way here, and there were hardly any true Japanese dogs left.

But wait, there was one. Saito blinked. Yes, there it was. An Akita. What looked to be a purebred Akita dog, wandering around the station. Oh my, he was beautiful. Saito went up to the dog.

He bent down and scratched its head.

"Hello, friend. You're a beauty, you know that? What are you doing here? Where's your owner?"

The dog barked.

"Will you take me to your owner?" Saito asked.

"If he does," the stationmaster said, who was standing behind them, "tell them to stop letting him come here every day. It's bothering the passengers."

"I think the only one it bothers is you!" a ticket-taking girl yelled. "Don't listen to him saying nasty things about that dog. He's very polite!"

"A polite mongrel," the stationmaster growled.

"He comes here every day?" Saito asked.

"Yes, every day at this time, he comes here and waits for the train. Then, after it leaves again, so does he. It's irritating,"

Saito raised his eyebrows. "He waits for the train?"

"Well," the stationmaster sighed, "I don't know. It's hard to know why dogs do what they do. But he comes every day right before the 3:00 p.m. train and leaves as soon as it leaves."

"It's so odd," said the ticket-taking girl, who had wandered out of her booth to join the conversation. "It really is like he's looking for someone who never comes."

The station was nearly empty now, and, as the stationmaster had said, the dog started to leave.

"Thank you!" Saito said quickly to both of them and chased after the dog. The creature led him to a normal-looking house with a man outside, watering plants.

"Hello," Saito said, "is this your dog?"

The man turned, setting down his watering can. "Hello there," he said. He looked at the dog. "Hachikō? Well, I guess he's kind of mine now. His owner died several months ago. I've looked after him ever since."

"He's a beautiful Akita. You don't see many purebred Akitas anymore."

"No," said the man, smiling as he tousled the dog's ears, "you sure don't. And he's a good dog. He and his former master were inseparable. He likes me all right, but I don't think he'll ever be as fond of anyone as he was of him."

"It seems he has a rather strange habit," Saito said, "of going to the train station every day."

"Oh yes," the man said. "He remembers."

"Remembers what?"

"Well, when his master was alive, he would walk to the station with Hachikō every day.

His master would get on the train, and Hachikō would walk home. Then his master would return on the 3:00 p.m. train every day, and Hachikō would be there waiting for him. Until one day," the man's face clouded, "his master wasn't able to come. He died very suddenly. But it doesn't seem that Hachikō understands. Even though it's been months, he keeps going to the station, waiting for Dr. Ueno to come and get him."

"Dr. Ueno?" Saito said. "Why, he was one of my teachers at the college. What a tragedy his death was."

110

"Yes," the man nodded. "I was his gardener. A tragedy indeed. But Hachikō keeps waiting for him. I wonder how long it will take for him to give up on it."

Hachikō didn't give up. He continued to go to the station in Shibuya every day. The commuters and workers at the station got so used to him, they started bringing him gifts and treats. Saito kept coming back to see Hachikō, and he published several articles about him. One of these catapulted the dog into national fame. He became a symbol of loyalty in Japan.

Hachikō continued to visit the station for more than nine years, only stopping when he died at age eleven. His pelt was stuffed and mounted, and it is still on display in the National Science Museum of Japan in Ueno, Tokyo. A statue of him was put up at the Shibuya Station, and there are two other statues of him in Japan and one in Rhode Island. A number of movies and children's books have been made about him. His ashes were buried next to his beloved master.

MOVING ROCKS

Brock sighed. Resting. This was what he liked. Just lying here, baking in the sun, watching the world around him change without effort, trouble, or movement. This was what a rock's life was supposed to be.

He'd hated that tumble down from the ridge. He'd felt it coming, the shifting of his foundations, the chipping away of what held him in place. It had been the most pain he'd ever experienced, and then it grew worse, filling him with terror. The creaking and slow giving away as he broke free, torn from his home of centuries to fall and fall, clattering, crumbling, falling to pieces, pain, pain, pain.

He was smaller now than he'd ever been, just a remnant of what he'd been on the ridge. But at least he was still. He'd never have to break free again. The ground here was flat, and there was nothing and nobody to disturb him. He'd keep sitting here. Forever.

"Hey, how's it going?"

Brock looked around. There was another rock, a large one, about twenty feet from him. He'd seen her before, but he could have sworn she used to be farther away. Odd. Regardless, he had no desire to reach out. Who needed friends when you were a rock?

"I'm Mok," the rock said.

"Hi," said Brock, not wishing to keep the conversation going.

"You're lucky to be here," Mok said.

"Why?" said Brock. "I much preferred my place on the ridge."

"Well, down here we get to move."

"What?"

"Yeah. I've traveled 1000 feet since I fell from the ridge a few centuries ago."

"No!" Brock moaned. "I hate moving. I've only done it one time, and it hurt so badly."

"Aw, it's not so bad," said Mok. "The change of view is actually quite nice. And the moving itself is a blast."

"No," Brock insisted. "There is nothing good about moving. I hate it now. I will hate it forever."

Mok chucked. "Forever's a long time to hate, Brock. Might as well learn to enjoy instead."

Brock grunted. "I hope I move away from you."

"But I might chase you!" Mok said. Her laughter resounded through the valley, and Brock ignored her for a very long time.

Death Valley, located in the Mojave Desert in California, is known as the hottest place on earth. Furnace Creek within the valley once reached a temperature of 134 degrees Fahrenheit, the hottest outdoor air temperature ever recorded. However, Death Valley has a few other quirks as well. It's home to the famous sailing stones.

The stones were first recognized by scientists in 1915 on what is now known as Racetrack Playa. The rocks leave behind trails on the desert floor, showing their progress. Scientists were mystified by the rocks' movements along a dry, desert floor.

Several hypotheses were proposed. The playa did get rain sometimes. Perhaps strong winds propelled the rocks across the mud? The huge size (one was estimated to be perhaps 700 pounds) of some of the rocks made this difficult to believe. Were the rocks sliding downhill? Unlikely since the land is incredibly flat. Were people or animals moving them? Was it the result of an earthquake or magnetism? Were supernatural forces involved?

In 2013, the mystery was solved as researchers arrived on premises at exactly the right time to watch the phenomenon. The playa had a few inches of water on it at the time, and in the cold winter night, the water froze. As the temperatures warmed in the morning, sheets of ice being propelled by the wind started to push the rocks around through the mud.

Some of the rocks were pushed quite far, and, over the course of a month, some were moved many different times. These circumstances were very rare, explaining why the rocks also tend to move so rarely.

Brock was cold. The ice frozen around him was colder than anything he'd ever experienced.

"Don't worry," Mok said. "It'll start melting soon. Then the fun will begin."

She was right about something beginning, though Brock wasn't sure he would call it fun. As he started to thaw, a breeze blew through the valley, pushing the sheets of ice around. As they moved, they pushed Brock, too.

He was frightened at first, expecting the pain he'd experienced when he'd fallen from the ridge. But it wasn't like that. The movement was slow and gentle. He slid easily through the mud. The squish of it made him giggle despite himself.

"See," Mok said, who had indeed moved closer to him when she'd been pushed by the ice. "It's fun, isn't it?"

And as the sun rose over Death Valley, Brock couldn't help but admire a view he'd never seen before.

THE LARGEST ORCHESTRA YOU'VE EVER SEEN

Sanouk and Virote walked slowly through the conservation center. Their parents had heard about the good work being done here, and they just had to come. So far, though, the children couldn't see anything being conserved other than the perfectly cut grass.

"How many elephants are supposed to be here?" Sanouk asked.

"I heard they had more than fifty," her father said.

"Fifty," Virote said. "That's kind of a lot of enormous creatures. So... where are they?"

"Be patient," his mother said. "We will see them soon."

A strange sound echoed through the grounds. It sounded like drums, gongs, and a marimba. Was that a harmonica?

"It sounds like the music from the temple," Sanouk said.

Virote turned to his father. "Do they play music for the elephants?"

His father smiled. "Ah, this is part of why I wanted to come. Be patient, Virote. You will see in time."

Then they were in a huge clearing, and there were elephants. Ten of them, grouped in a sort of semicircle around a collection of instruments.

"Oh," Sanouk said, "they don't play music for the elephants, the elephants play music for them."

And they were. One elephant rhythmically beat two drums with his trunk. Another held a stick to beat a marimba. Another also used a stick to beat a number of different-sized gongs. And another, yes, blew through a harmonica grasped in its trunk.

"What is this?" Virote said.

"They call it an elephant orchestra," his mother said, grinning. "Ooh, look at that one scraping the stick along his instrument. He looks so happy."

"But ... it's not really music," Virote said. "They're just having fun."

"Ah," his father said, tousling his hair, "but what else do musicians do?"

Virote looked on, puzzled.

Because of studies done with certain elephants showing that they were capable of painting, some researchers wondered if they could also play music.

David Sulzer, neuroscientist and experimental musician, and Richard Lair, an elephant expert, decided to see if they could make it happen. Thus, the Thai Elephant Orchestra was formed at the Thai Elephant Conservation Center.

The two men worked together to create enormous instruments that were basically indestructible. As Sulzer put it, with elephants involved, "Even a little hit would break a regular instrument into smithereens." They also had to pick instruments that could be played with an elephant's trunk or with a stick held in the trunk. By 2000, the men were ready to start forming their group of music-playing elephants.

Sulzer thought training the elephants would be difficult. "I thought that we'd have to give them a banana every time they hit it and an apple every time they made a note," he said. "But it was nothing like that—I would play it, hand them the stick, and that was it. They were playing in a few minutes." Indeed, some enjoyed the process so much that it was hard to get them to stop.

It's long been known among Thai elephant keepers, that elephants enjoy music.

They would play or sing to the elephants to calm them or just to make them happy. However, the orchestra wasn't just formed to give the elephants joy or show their ability to play. Lair, who worked at the conservation center, believed it could be a good tourist attraction, drawing more funding for the center.

Though elephants have long been an important animal symbolically in Thailand, their numbers have dwindled at a horrible rate.

The number of Asian elephants in Thailand about a hundred years ago was around 100,000. Around 2000, the numbers had dropped to 3,000-4,000 making them endangered.

Places like the conservation center want to bring people awareness of the elephants' plight and draw in donations for them. This was why Sulzer recorded CDs of the elephants to sell. These songs are still available on Spotify, Apple Music, Pandora, and Apple Music.

"But is it really music?" Virote insisted.

One of the workers looked at him and grinned. "Oh, they know what they're doing. Look at their rhythm. And those who trained them at one point put bad notes on the instruments to see if the elephants cared if they were in tune. The elephants started avoiding those notes. So yes, I think it's really music."

"Weird," Virote said.

"Why should we have the monopoly on the music kingdom just because we're humans?" Sanouk said. "Music is all over creation! Just listen to birds. Why not elephants, too?"

"Why not," her father said, clapping her on the shoulder. "Why not indeed?"

UNLIKELY FRIENDS

"Mama!" the baby hippo cried, jumping behind the ancient tortoise. "Mama, I've missed you so much. I've been so scared."

The tortoise hissed at the hippo. "What are you talking about, you disrespectful whippersnapper. You get away from me." He moved away.

The hippo followed. "Mama, what are you doing? Are we playing a game? Am I supposed to follow you?"

"Stop it, you young nincompoop! Get away from me!"

"Yay! I love this game!" The hippo continued to chase the tortoise around and around and around ...

The Kenyan town of Malindi experienced many seasons with heavy rains, but the December of 2004 stood out in particular. The high waters brought some unexpected visitors. A pod of hippos had drifted down the bloated Sabaki River to Malindi's Indian Ocean coast.

The villagers were not thrilled with the hippos' arrival. Hippos are one of the most dangerous animals in Africa, killing about 500 people a year. They tried to herd them back up the river, but the hippos liked eating the grasses in the villagers' yards and along the shore. And it's hard to persuade an 8,000-pound, cantankerous creature to do anything it doesn't want to. Unfortunately, this turned out to be fatal for most of the hippo pod.

On December 26, 2004, the Indian Ocean Tsunami decimated coastlands in Indonesia, Sri Lanka, Thailand, and India. It then traveled across the ocean and struck the coast of Africa. This included the town of Malindi.

Following the tsunami, the villagers were too busy cleaning up the town wreckage to worry about the hippos. When they finally did check, they found only one baby hippo, less than a year old, was left, stranded on a reef far from the shore. The villagers went to work trying to rescue him.

This was not an easy feat. Though the hippo was a baby, he weighed 600 pounds, and he was terrified. He broke the fishing nets they tried to use to drag him to shore.

They returned with heavier-duty shark nets, and succeeded in netting him only after a young man threw himself on the hippo, wrestling him until the net was secured. The young man's name was Owen. They named baby Owen after him.

After they'd gotten the baby hippo into a truck bed, they called the Haller Park sanctuary in Bamburi, Kenya. Workers set out to pick him up.

Though Owen put up another huge fight, they managed to get him to the sanctuary eventually. He was put in a habitat with several other animals. One of these animals was a huge, 130-year-old Aldabra tortoise named Mzee. When Owen saw the tortoise, he ran to him, hiding behind him as baby hippos often do with their mothers when they're frightened.

Mzee was not happy about this, and he hissed at Owen and moved away. But tortoises aren't that fast (if you haven't heard), and the baby hippo continued to follow Mzee around. Mzee eventually got used to Owen, and thus began a longstanding friendship that would flummox the most intelligent of scientists.

Owen followed Mzee all over the place and tried to get the tortoise to go on walks with him. Mzee was usually solitary, which is typical for Aldabra tortoises. Surprisingly though, he started to follow the baby hippo. Owen started to eat again alongside Mzee, feeling safe near his friend. The two swam together. They slept together. They started to rub noses and show each other affection.

This relationship confused scientists. They thought that Mzee's round shape and hippo-like coloring might have made Owen see him as a mother-figure. Hippos depend on their mothers to survive for the first four years of their lives, so Owen needed someone to depend on.

As for why Mzee put up with Owen, scientists have no clue. Mzee could have attacked Owen. This would've made sense. Aldabra tortoises can do major damage. But he never did. These tortoises occasionally live in groups, so perhaps Mzee got Owen confused with another tortoise (though it seems unlikely for a creature so old and wise).

Perhaps Mzee could see that the hippo was young and needed him, so he took pity. Perhaps Mzee just chose to like Owen since he couldn't get rid of him. Regardless, they got along. And it was adorable to watch the two together.

After a few years, Owen got too big to continue living with Mzee, and they moved him into another enclosure with a female hippo named Cleo. The two bonded easily. Mzee returned to his solitude. The two still live together in Haller Park, happily, though separate now.

A MYSTERY OR FAKE NEWS?

"Jorge, have you seen my purple sneakers?" Emelina asked.

Jorge didn't look away from the screen. "Emelina, I'm trying to make Maple's dream vacation home. I can't be distracted right now."

Emelina rolled her eyes. "I think Maple can wait three seconds, Jorge."

"Nope. I'll get bad customer reviews because of my slow service."

"Jorge, where are my shoes?"

Jorge finally turned to her and sighed. "What?"

"Where are my shoes?!"

"Your shoes? How should I know?"

Emelina said, "I don't know. I've looked everywhere, so I've had to resort to asking you."

Jorge turned back to his game. "Oh, I don't know. They're probably at the bottom of the Bermuda Triangle."

"What the heck are you even talking about?"

"Ignorant little sister. The Bermuda Triangle is where stuff goes to disappear. It's like where a bunch of boats and planes have disappeared and stuff."

"You're making this up."

"Nope. It's totally a thing. Go look it up. Educate yourself."

"Sure. I'll go educate myself by finding my shoes. You get back to helping Maple."

"Already on it."

The Bermuda Triangle, a region in the Atlantic that's sometimes said to be between the three corners of Miami, Florida; San Juan, Puerto Rico; and Bermuda.

There has been a mystery attached to this area in the ocean since 1950 when a man named Edward Van Winkle Jones wrote an article entitled, "Sea's Puzzles Still Baffle Men in Pushbutton Age."

Jones, though he doesn't use the name "Bermuda Triangle," outlined four different disappearances, one with a boat, three involving aircraft in which the vehicles and their passengers, "disappear[ed] without a trace."

Other articles followed, telling of the same disappearances and others in the same vicinity. George Sand's article in the 1952 October edition of Fate was the first to outline the triangle's corners and to suggest that perhaps supernatural forces were to blame for these strange vanishings. This was followed by still more articles, and they did sound eerie. Boats and planes went missing in this region. The writers suggested explanations involving the lost island of Atlantis, alternate dimensions, UFOs, and more. Was there actually something going on just north of the Caribbean? Was it safe to travel there?

Then came a new series of articles to combat these supernatural explanations. Larry Kusche wrote an entire book to debunk these ideas. He claimed that those writing about the mysteries of the Bermuda Triangle were exaggerating, leaving out important information, and straight out spreading false information.

Firstly, the waters of the Bermuda Triangle are frequently traveled. The number of ships and aircraft disappearing in this section is comparable to the proportion that disappear in other parts of the ocean. This region isn't exceptional. In fact, according to a report put out by the World Wide Fund for Nature, in the world's top ten most dangerous waters to travel over, the Bermuda Triangle didn't make the list.

Tropical tornados also travel over the sea in this region, which can take down ships and planes with very little warning. Though some of these disappearances were attributed to such bad weather, many of the writers portrayed the disappearances as having happened on blue-sky, sunny days.

In addition, some of the reports of disappearances simply didn't happen. One writer spoke of a disappearance of a plane in the Bermuda Triangle when the plane crashed off Daytona Beach with hundreds of people watching.

Other writers said boats disappeared that actually made it to port, just a bit late.

One ship was said to have been lost in the Atlantic when it was really lost in the Pacific, and on and on. In short, there was a lot of sloppy research and trying to make things sound mysterious that weren't. Is it dangerous to travel in the Bermuda Triangle? Not so very much more than it is to travel over the ocean in general. And really, you're at a higher risk every time you take a ride on the freeway.

"Liar!" Emelina threw one of her purple Nikes at Jorge.

"Hey!" Jorge dropped his controller. "Geez, what are you talking about?"

"I looked up the Bermuda Triangle, and it's not even that dangerous! The article said people have been making up stupid stuff about how weird and mysterious it is for decades, but it's not actually weird or mysterious. It's just a normal place on the sea, which means ships sink sometimes and planes go down sometimes! You're trying to make me dumber by telling me lies!" She threw her other shoe at him. Jorge covered his face with his arms.

"Gosh, stop it! Good grief, Emelina, I didn't know. I was just telling you what I'd heard."

"Well," Emelina said, crossing her arms, "what you heard was wrong. Next time, make sure you're teaching your little sister the truth, not lies. Before you teach, you should know what the heck you're talking about." She stalked out of the room.

Jorge sighed. "Little sisters." He picked up his controller again. "Don't worry, Maple. I've got you."

DESERT DRAWINGS

The sun slanted through the window and laid gentle fingers across Raven's sketchbook as she shaded and shaped the images. A knock shattered her serenity, and she groaned.

"Don't come in," she said.

The door opened, and Cass stuck her head in. "Knock, knock."

"I said don't come in." Raven's eyes were glued to her sketchbook once more.

"I know, but no one else is here, and I'm bored." She flopped on the floor next to Raven's bed, resting her head on the quilt. "What 'cha drawing?"

"What does it look like?" Raven spoke through gritted teeth.

"Hmmm," Cass tapped her chin. "A bird of some sort. Or, no, a few birds. And their wings are outstretched, so are they flying?"

Raven didn't answer.

"Hey, Rave, I was reading this book today about an ancient Peruvian people who liked to draw, too. They drew these enormous pictures of plants and animals in the desert that have been preserved for hundreds, maybe thousands of years."

Raven still didn't answer.

"They're actually pretty cool-looking. Want to see?" Cass dug a book out of her backpack and flipped it open, laying it next to Raven's sketchpad. Raven glanced at it. Then she looked for longer.

"Those are kind of cool," Raven said.

"I know, right! And some people think they were drawn by aliens or something."

"What?"

"But I think they were probably just made by people like you. People who like to create beautiful pictures."

Raven looked at Cass with a softer expression. "Thanks, Cass."

"You can read it, if you want."

Raven's gaze returned to the book. She started to read.

The Nazca lines are estimated to have been made in the southern deserts of Peru between the years 200 BC and 600 AD. Due to the dry, calm climate, the lines have lasted for centuries.

Some of the strokes are long, road-like lines, one of them running as far as thirty miles, but there are also several distinct shapes. These include a hummingbird, a monkey, a tree, and a human-like giant nicknamed "the astronaut." The largest of these shapes is 400 yards long, with the lines being one to six feet wide. They were made by the Nazca people, but the reasons for the creation have puzzled historians for the past ninety years.

The lines were noticed a few times throughout history, but they were originally thought to be ancient roads. It wasn't until 1927 when Toribio Mejia Xesspe was hiking through the Peruvian foothills that he realized the lines actually made pictures. He saw not just roads but intricate shapes. As other investigators flew in to study the lines, they were able to get a better look at them from their aircraft.

Some people came up with interesting theories regarding the lines' creation. Some said they couldn't have been made by ancient people unless the people had been able to fly, and there was speculation about aliens being involved. These rumors were amplified by the astronaut figure, which had an enormous head. Some people thought this was an alien. However, scholars think the image is just a cartoonish drawing with certain features amplified. This is characteristic of the other Nazca images.

Aliens weren't needed to help make the lines, either. The process was actually quite simple. Scholars believe that the Nazca created these shapes by raking back the top layer of red rocks to show the lighter-colored sand beneath. They could have drawn small versions of the shapes and used stakes (some of which have been found in the area) and ropes to scale the images up.

Why did the Nazca go to all this trouble, though? Some thought the shapes and lines were a giant calendar, showing how the heavenly bodies moved throughout the year. Others thought at least some of them were, in fact, used as roads. Others thought the lines were irrigation systems, others that they were used for religious rituals, others still that they were there to alert extraterrestrial life of a safe landing zone. What's the truth? Perhaps a combination of all of these (well, except perhaps the last one).

Raven looked back up at Cass. "That is some weird stuff."

"I know, right. And I know what you're drawing now. It's a flock of ravens, isn't it? A bit self-obsessed there, sis?"

Raven punched her in the arm.

"It's good, though."

Raven smiled. "Thanks. Not as cool as what those Nazca people did."

"Eh, you're young," Cass said. "You've still got time to do your great work."

"Thanks, sis."

"Anytime."

"Now get out of my room."

Cass sighed. "Okay."

CODE OR WISECRACK??

Artemis yawned. She hated museums. And libraries. Yale's Beinecke Rare Book and Manuscript Library was kind of like a mixture of both.

"Look at this, Artie!" her friend James said, goggling at some moldy old book through the glass.

"What?" she asked.

"It's the Gutenberg Bible! This is one of the very first books ever printed on a movable-type printing press back in the 1400s. That invention changed the world forever."

Artemis nodded and sighed. "Yeah. Made it so we'll never be allowed to stop reading books."

"Why would you want to?" James asked, his eyes still glued to the glass.

Artemis didn't answer. She wandered past him to glance at a book in another glass case. This one had a lot of pictures in it, and it didn't seem to be written in English. She read the little plaque next to it "Voynich Manuscript." And, having nothing better to do, she decided to read on.

The Voynich Manuscript is estimated to have been written in the 15th or 16th century. It uses a code that cryptographers call Voynichese. People have been trying to crack the code for the last one hundred years, but none have succeeded.

The book is separated into six sections: the first is about plant life and contains a great many pictures of plants, most of which scholars can't identify. The second section is astrological, containing Zodiac signs and astral charts. The third is therapeutic bathing, containing many pictures of women sitting in baths or pools, some with crowns, interacting with metal tubes and pipes. The fourth section is pharmaceutical, showing pictures of plants and roots used for medical purposes. The last section is mostly just text and may be composed of recipes.

As soon as Artemis read about the strange pictures of the ladies bathing, she laughed out loud and pulled out her phone. She Googled images of the Voynich Manuscript, and her laughter didn't stop.

"What's so funny?" James asked, tearing himself away from a nearby display of the 1,300-year-old Japanese scroll. Artemis showed him her phone, still giggling.

James didn't smile. "Artie, we're here to learn, not look at weird drawings on the internet."

"The weird drawings are from one of these books you want to learn about, dearest James."

"What?"

Artemis showed him the display. While he read it, she continued to read more about the Voynich Manuscript on her phone. Apparently, it was named after the man who had bought it in 1912, a rare book seller named Wilfrid Voynich. He thought it was written by an intellectual friar in the Middle Ages named Roger Bacon. Scholars don't believe this, though, and just like the language inside, there is much debate about the book's authorship. Some thought Voynich himself might have written it, using the knowledge he'd acquired in the rare book trade.

The greatest cryptographers in history tried to crack the code of the Voynich Manuscript for a century, some studying it for forty years or more. It's not simple symbolic language where symbols are substituted for letters. There may be a type of abbreviation used, substituting shorthand for normal words, and then using a cypher to complicate it further. Some think that anagrams are employed. Other scholars gave up deciphering the code at all and say there is no comprehensible language in it. Someone just wrote a bunch of gibberish and drew some weird pictures, trying to pass it off as historically significant. The whole thing is no more than a hoax.

Artemis laughed again. "Good grief, I really hope it's a bunch of nonsense!"

"But look," James was staring at the Voynich Manuscript now, "maybe if you took the first letter of each word and put them together …"

"That's an anagram," Artemis said. "They've already tried it."

"Still, I wonder …" James kept staring.

Artemis stood next to him and then punched him hard in the arm.

"Ow! Why'd you do that?" James looked wounded and rubbed his arm.

"Bringing you back to the real world. Don't waste your time," Artemis said. "If geniuses have been trying to figure this out for one hundred years, you're not going to figure it out. Go find something useful to do with your time."

James's nose went up. "I could be the one to figure it out. I could be the one to go down in history as the one who cracked the Voynich code."

Artemis grinned a wicked grin. "If I go down in history, I want to be remembered as the person who wrote a bunch of gibberish and kept brainiacs like you busy for a century trying to figure it out when it never meant anything at all."

SMEAR ME WITH POO AND MAKE ME A MAN

Kidus woke earlier than anyone else in his family. He had slept poorly. He was too excited, too nervous. He stepped over his brothers and sisters to reach the door. He watched the sun rise over termite mounds and Joshua trees. Today was the day he could become a man. If he did it right. If he managed not to fall.

His father had given him his boko a week ago. He had spent three days traveling to the homes of his family, handing out the marked ropes. He showed them his boko and invited them to come and take part in the ritual.

A hand clapped down on Kidus's shoulder. "Are you ready, my son?"

"I hope so, Father."

"We will see, Kidus. We will see. I believe you are ready, though. I would not have given you your boko if I did not."

"Thank you, Father."

"Your mother is getting ready. She will want you soon. She will want to be part of the scrubbing. If anything must be scrubbed, your mother wants to do it." His father grinned.

"Yes, Father."

"Kidus," the man tipped his son's chin up so the boy had to meet his eyes, "do not be afraid. Fear makes you weak. It will not make you a man."

"Yes, Father."

The Hamer people, who live in the Omo Valley in south-western Ethiopia, hold a common ritual. It is performed when a father decides his son is old enough to become a man. The boy's father will give him a short stick, a boko, to tell him that it is time to have the ritual.

The boy will then travel to his relatives, showing them his boko and distributing specially marked ropes. The ropes are marked as a way for the relatives to know when the ceremony will be held. Since the Hamer people don't use a calendar, they use ropes, cutting off a piece of it every day at the marked places. When the rope runs out, they know that it's the day of the ritual.

On the chosen day, guests arrive, and the boy's family treats them to drinks. The women dress up in traditional garb and wear bells on their legs. They begin to dance and play horns.

As sunset approaches, the boy strips off his clothes and has his head shaved. He is then scrubbed with sand to wash away his sins. To top it all, they smear him with dung to strengthen him and strap pieces of bark on him for spiritual help.

Then, he is led to face the bulls. Seven to ten bulls are lined up in a row and smeared with dung to make them slippery. The boy is supposed to jump onto the bulls' backs, run across, and jump back down four times without falling. If he succeeds, he's a man. If he fails, he has to wait a year to go through the ritual again. None of his younger brothers can go through the ritual until he passes.

When the young man succeeds, his people cheer for him and blast their horns. A piece of animal hide is strapped around his neck, and his relatives continue to celebrate with him into the wee hours of the morning. He is now a man, able to be married and own his own cattle.

Kidus stared up at the line of bulls, so tall, so strong, so slick with dung. But this was not the first time he'd done this. He'd known his day would been soon, and he'd been practicing with his father's bulls. He jumped and ran, jumped and ran, jumped and ran, jumped and ran. Four times. Not a fall. His heart was racing and also soaring. He threw his fist in the air as his family cheered.

His father clapped him on the shoulder. "You are now a Maza, my son, a man."

Kidus smiled hugely at his father.

His father turned to the family and shouted, "Let the celebration begin!" The people roared in approval.

DEEP AND SAFE

Ella slowly flapped her way along the bottom of the sea. It was safe down here. It was quiet. She could reflect, eat, and not worry about danger. She could peacefully search until she found a nice place to lay her eggs.

She had a few ready to lay, and she was going to take good care of them. She'd met updwellers a few times, fish who had gotten lost and wandered down here to the deepest deep. They'd told her of the cruelty of the shallow world. Up there, they didn't always accept you for who you were. They liked to make fun of things that were different. Also, they liked to eat you up there. Not for her. And not for her children. They would stay safe in the deep.

The dumbo octopus lives deeper in the ocean than any other octopus, making their home along the ocean floor at between about 1,000-13,000 feet beneath sea-level. The lowest scientists have ever seen one was 20,000 feet below.

Most of them are pretty small, measuring only 8-12 inches long, but one was once found that was a whoppy 5 feet 10 inches. They normally live 3-5 years. They live in the deep all over the world, having been discovered off the coast of Oregon, the Philippines, New Zealand, Australia, California, Mexico, Norway, Papua, and New Guinea.

Dumbo octopuses are different in many ways. Named after the elephant that uses his ears to fly in the Disney movie, these mollusks have ear-like "wings" (fins really) located above each of their eyes. They use the fins to propel themselves forward. They are also umbrella octopuses, which means that their tentacles are webbed together, and they use these tentacles to steer. The little ear-winged umbrella mollusks are actually pretty cute.

Dumbo octopuses live so deep in the ocean that they have few predators. They're in so little need of protection that they have neither the ink sacks most octopuses use to defend themselves nor do they have the camouflage skills many other octopuses use to blend into their surroundings and hide.

Scientists presume that sharks, seals, and sperm whales might eat these creatures, but only the shark has been found with a Dumbo octopus in its stomach.

They also remain pretty much completely unbothered by human society, being far too deep for us to come into contact with them often.

Their lives are rather peaceful. They drift along, looking for crustaceans, plankton, and bristle worms to eat. Instead of crushing and breaking up their food like most octopuses, Dumbo octopuses are able to swallow it whole.

They also don't hang out much with others of their kind. The females receive portable fertilization packets from the males, which they can carry along for long periods of time until they find suitable places to lay their eggs.

Unlike many other types of octopuses, Dumbo octopuses don't hang out after laying their eggs to guard them or keep them warm. The mother lays her eggs, fertilizes them with the packet she got from the male, and moves on. When the octopuses hatch, they're developed and intelligent enough to strike out on their own.

They're different from the conventional octopus in many ways, but hey, in the deepest depths of the sea, most creatures are pretty weird. And there aren't really enough of them to mind it very much.

She continued to swim, looking for the perfect place to lay her eggs. Ah, there it was. A long growth of deep-sea coral. It looked sturdy. Nothing would bother her children here.

Gently, quietly, she placed her eggs in a little divot of the coral. Fertilizing them with the fertilization packet she'd gotten from a male a few months ago, she looked down at them tenderly.

"Come to life, little ones," she said. "It will be a quiet, peaceful life. You will be unbothered. You are unlikely to face any ridicule or danger. You will be safe. I wish you well, my children."

And with that, she flapped her little ear-fins and swam away.

THE SHIP MOORED IN ICE

"How long have you been staring at this screen?" the scientist asked. The oceanographer was looking slightly bug-eyed.

"Six hours," he said. "I don't have the hard job, though."

"No, that's mine," said his companion, the engineer. "I get to drive a remote-control boat through Antarctic ice water, making sure I don't hit any of the carnage that's been sunk in this deathtrap of a sea for the last however many millennia."

"How many dives have you done so far?" the scientist asked.

"Thirty," the engineer replied.

"Do you really think we'll ever find it?"

The engineer and oceanographer didn't look at her, both of their eyes still glued to the screen. "I don't know," the oceanographer said. "There's a lot of sea to search. I sure hope so though."

"Do you think there'll be anything left?" the scientist asked.

Neither answered. The oceanographer kept on searching the screen. The engineer kept on steering the underwater vehicle. They continued their quest to find the Endurance, the vessel that had sunk 106 years before on an Antarctic exploration.

Ernest Shackleton had led the mission in a quest to travel across Antarctica for the first time. His plan was to sail the Endurance down to Vahsel Bay in the Weddell Sea and then trek across the continent to a ship on the other side. The idea greatly excited the public. Shackleton had experience in Antarctic exploration, and there was confidence in his ability to succeed.

He received most of his funding from private donors, and 5,000 people applied to join his mission.

Shackleton set out from England in August of 1914, heading down to South Georgia Island, an island located southeast of the tip of South America and one of Antarctica's closest neighbors. The Imperial Trans-Antarctic Expedition departed South Georgia on December 5, 1914, sailing out into the Weddell Sea.

Shackleton quickly found that there were many more ice packs to maneuver than they expected. The Endurance made her way around them as much as she could, but, eventually, she got stuck.

The crew waited, trying to dig the ship free at first and then giving up and camping out. Shackleton thought they'd be able to get the ship free after the winter months which, in Antarctica, means May, June, and July. However, the spring thaws that followed pushed the expanding ice into the Endurance, dealing her a mortal blow that October. Shackleton ordered his crew to abandon ship, and the Endurance sank beneath the ice.

Shackleton managed to keep his men alive and sail three lifeboats to Elephant Island, 346 miles away from where the Endurance sank. From there, Shackleton and five of the men sailed 720 miles on one of the lifeboats to South Georgia, a journey that is legendarily dangerous to this day.

Shackleton later returned to Elephant Island and the Weddell Sea to retrieve the rest of his crew. Every single member lived through this experience. Well, every part of the crew but their ship.

People wondered what had become of the sunken Endurance, but, as one can learn from Shackleton's journey, Antarctic exploration is no easy task, especially when seeking something at the bottom of a very deep sea. Scientists also weren't sure what would be left of the ship, not knowing how much of it had held together through its icy demise.

In 2022, the Agulhas II set out to look for the Endurance. She was manned by a crew of sixty-three engineers, geophysicists, doctors, statisticians, scientists, oceanographers, polar field guides, and more. They were doing many tasks on this mission: researching ice science, weather forecasting, doing marine engineering research, and gathering footage for educational resources. They were doing a lot. But their main mission was to find the Endurance.

On March 5, 2022, an eerie sight came on the screen of the Agulhas II. There was the Endurance. It had not only held together, but it was also in almost-perfect condition. The frigid waters had preserved the ship, making it look like it only sank yesterday and not 106 years ago. Like her captain and her name, she perseveres, even at the bottom of the sea.

THE FROZEN EARS PROBLEM

Chester took another lap around the pond on his skates. He loved the sound of the metal scraping on the ice, the wind rushing past his ears. Well, he loved the movement of the wind. But by the time he was finished, his ears were practically made of ice. Maine's icy weather was not kind to uncovered ears, and, as he slid to the side of the pond and sat on the bank, he sat and covered his ears with his hands.

His big sister slid to a stop in front of him. "Come on, Chester," she panted. "Let's go around again."

"I can't, Hettie. My ears are too cold."

She laughed at him. "Come on, Chester. Be a big boy and wear the hat Aunt Muriel made you." She pulled at the ear flaps on her hat that covered both her ears.

"I hate that hat," said Chester. "It makes my ears itch. I'd rather have cold ears than itchy ears."

"Well, it seems you can keep skating longer when you're itchy than when you're frozen," said Hettie, taking off again. "See you at home, Ice Ears."

The fifteen-year-old started home, thinking about the problem. Cold ears. Itchy ears. A person shouldn't have to choose. A person should be able to have ears that were both warm and comfortable.

When he got home, he dug around in the barn for a spool of farm wire. He cut it and twisted it into a couple of circles. Then he went inside. His grandmother was sitting in a rocking chair, darning a pair of thick, wool socks.

"Gram," he said, "could you sew something for me?"

Gram beamed up at him. "Anything for my grandbaby."

Chester decided it wasn't the right time to tell her not to call him a grandbaby.

"Could you sew some fur from that beaver pelt I got last weekend over these?" He showed her the circles he'd made from the farm wire.

"What on earth for, sweetie?"

"It's just an idea I had," said Chester.

She took his chin in her hand. "You always have lots of ideas, don't you, Chester? And I bet one day one of those ideas is going to take you somewhere amazing. Of course, I'll sew the fur for you."

"Thanks, Gram," Chester said, kissing her on the cheek.

The next day, Chester went skating again with wire circles covered with beaver fur. His ears stayed warm, though the warmers did slip around under his hat, and he had to keep adjusting them. When he came home, he fastened the two circles together with a wire that went over his head, keeping the warmers in place. Later, he added black velvet to the section that was on his ear to make it softer.

In 1877 at the age of eighteen, Chester Greenwood received a patent for his "champion ear protectors." Later, he changed the name to "earmuffs." Greenwood built a factory and, in six years, was making 30,000 pairs of earmuffs a year. The earmuffs grew in popularity and were in great demand for soldiers in World War I, with the factory then producing more than 400,000 pairs a year.

Greenwood continued to invent, gaining more than 100 patents by the end of his life. His ideas varied, including a steel-tooth rake, a wide-bottomed kettle, a donut hook, a folding bed, and a shock absorber design that is still used in airplane landing gear. He also had a bicycle business and introduced one of the first telephone systems to his hometown of Farmington.

He was active and well-loved in Farmington up to his death in 1937. In 1977, the state of Maine declared December 21st, often the first day of winter, to be Chester Greenwood Day. They hold a parade in his honor on the first Saturday of every December. All because his ears got cold.

THE DISCOVERY OF ICE ON A STICK

"I just wanna say," said Art, leaning back against the porch rail, "that they're gonna get clobbered."

"Destroyed," said Leroy.

"Absolutely slaughtered," said Davis.

"The scrawny pack of middle school basketball players we have on our team," said Art, "would be as likely to beat the Tigers from the Heights as an actual hornet has of beating a tiger."

"It could sting his paw," Leroy snickered.

"And the tiger would crush it right after," said Art.

"Well, you know what's the same about a game where our team loses and a game where our team wins?" asked Frank from his porch step.

"The number of possible customers," his three friends said in unison.

"Geez, Frank," said Davis, "when you gonna stop spending your free time selling stuff? You're supposed to have fun at a basketball game."

"Selling stuff is fun," Frank said, stirring a flavor packet into his water and taking a sip. "It leads to money, and who doesn't think money is fun?"

"You love selling stuff so much," said Leroy, "soon you're gonna start selling your money." He laughed again, shaking the porch swing he and Davis were sharing.

Davis smacked him on the back of his head. "Stop shaking the swing like that. It's irritating."

Leroy thumbed his nose at him, and Davis smacked his head again.

"All right, all right," said Art, hopping down from the porch railing. "Enough. Let's go ride to Erickson's and get a soda."

He didn't have to say it twice. The boys were off the porch in a minute, hooting and hollering at each other, Leroy chasing Davis who had stolen his hat. Their bikes hit the street, and the sound of their clicking gears faded into the distance.

Frank's cup of flavored water sat on the porch, forgotten, the stirring stick he'd used to mix it poking out like a kitten's head from a shoebox.

Frank stayed out with his friends until dusk, and he didn't see his glass in the fading light. That night, it was extremely cold for the Los Angeles area, the temperature dropping several degrees below freezing.

The next morning, as Frank stepped out of his house to wait for the school bus, he noticed the cup. When he picked it up, he realized the liquid had frozen solid. He also realized that he could pull the chunk of ice out using the stirrer he'd left in it, leaving him with a large chunk of ice on a stick. Frank gave it a lick. It tasted strongly of the flavoring packet he'd mixed in.

As Frank climbed onto the bus, he carried the ice on a stick with him. He took his seat next to Art.

"Try this," he said, handing it to Art.

"Try it?" Art said. "You want me to break my teeth on a block of ice? No thanks, Franky boy."

"No, don't bite it," said Frank. "Lick it."

Art raised his eyebrows at him, but he did as he was told. "Hey, that's not too bad."

"That's what I thought!" Frank said. "It's good, right?"

"Let me try," said Davis, poking his head over the top of the seat.

"Naw, me!" said Leroy, shoving Davis aside. Leroy grabbed it, and the two tussled. Leroy managed to get his tongue on the waving ice pop. "Hey, that's good, Frank!"

"I know," said Frank. "I know."

"Oh boy, here we go," said Art.

"What?" asked Frank.

"Something else for you to sell," said Art.

Frank just smiled and stared out the window, thinking of all the people who would be hot in the coming warm months, and how refreshing a nice block of ice on a stick would be. It looked like an upside-down icicle.

"Epsicle," Frank whispered. "That's what I'll call them."

"Yeah," said Art. "Like your last name mixed with icicle. That's kinda cool."

"Yeah," said Frank. "Yeah, it is."

Frank Epperson started selling "Epsicles" to kids in his neighborhood. As his business grew, he started selling them at Neptune Beach, an amusement park near his home. The ice pop was well-liked, and in 1924, when Epperson was a grown man, he patented the idea. His children influenced him to change the name to "Pop's Sicle." The name stuck. Though Popsicle is a brand name for ice pops, it's become a household term. All because young Frank forgot to clear up his dishes.

CONCLUSION

These short stories have shown us that real life can sometimes be more strange than any made-up story. The weird and wonderful accounts we've read remind us that there's still so much out there we don't know. Every story in this book and in these bonus chapters tell us that unexpected or amazing things can happen at any time, any day, and anywhere.

In fact, there are amazing new stories happening right now. Somewhere a new discovery is being made, someone is overcoming a challenge that will inspire others, maybe a new genius like Einstein is being born or taking his or her first steps right this moment. Who knows, but this world is wild, and so many more incredible stories are yet to happen.

From the bizarre to the beautiful, you've read your way through tales that show how extraordinary our world can be.

Now, I invite you to be part of our story by leaving a quick review. It will only take a few seconds and can be just a couple words. As a family-run business, each review helps us.

So, grab your phone, scan that QR code, and let me know what you thought of *Captivating Stories for Curious Kids*!

CLAIM YOUR FREE GIFT!

Get instant access to the
exclusive chapters and audio!

THIS ISN'T AVAILABLE ANYWHERE ELSE!

Scan the QR code below with your phone
camera now to get your gift!

Made in the USA
Columbia, SC
14 December 2024

2777a520-6426-4ad4-a92a-7391adcdcaafR01